LOST HOUSES

IN & AROUND WREXHAM

Published by

Guidelines Books & Sales
11 Belmont Road, Ipstones, Stoke on Trent ST10 2JN
Tel: 07971 990 649
Email: author.porter@gmail.com

ISBN: 978-1-84306-396-4

Printed by Information Press Ltd, Eynsham, Oxford

Front cover: Broughton Hall, Worthenbury; **Back cover top:** Brymbo Hall; **bottom:** Chester Street House
Page 1: Horsley Hall; **Title page:** Brymbo Hall; **Above:** Drawing room, Horsley Hall

LOST HOUSES
IN & AROUND WREXHAM

Raymond Lowe

CONTENTS

PREFACE

It has given me great pleasure and enjoyment – to compile these historical notes, and search for the photographs of those forgotten, but interesting houses that once graced the landscape in and around the Wrexham area. It is sad to see so many of those historical buildings of architectural interest disappear from the countryside, lost for ever; only the history of the families who at one time lived in them remains. One might say that this type of dwelling has had its day, and served the purpose for which the structure had been built. These properties had become no longer economical to maintain financially, or to obtain the staff to run them under present day conditions. It is surprising to note how many historical buildings in both urban and rural areas have been removed during the twentieth century in the Wrexham area. These have been not only domestic buildings but other structures, such as the old Town Hall, which once stood at the top of Townhill.

One might say that some of these historical buildings are not attractive in design, like some we see on our travels, but they are unique, and a good example of the type of building one could find of their period. It would have been of great value to the community and the town if an alternative use could have been found, so that something of our past heritage could be handed down to the next generation.

Those properties had been built with a high standard of materials. To this was added the skill of the tradesman of those bygone days: the carpenter and the stonemasons who carried out intricate craftsmanship with the crude working tools of their trade. The plasterers executed ornamental ceilings and walls the like of which we will never see again. We in the building trade to-day, with all the sophisticated tools at our disposal, should take off our hats to their skill. In those days a boy, on leaving school, was apprenticed to a trade with a building firm. He served seven years learning his trade. He worked on the building site where he saw the building grow from a hole in the ground to completion, he came in contact with the other trades on site, receiving a wide experience. Today the boy receives his training in the class room in one of the technical colleges and his outlook on his trade is limited.

I can give an example of this – just before I retired from my profession of a building surveyor. My firm was developing a corner site of which I was carrying out the supervision. We required two bricklayers to complete the building of the brick perimeter wall to the boundary of the site. The concrete foundations had already been cast for the wall which had a specification of 9 inches thick and 4 feet high, finished with brick-on-edge coping and joints to be weathered pointed. Two young men arrived on site one morning who were in their early twenties. I explained what was required and the foreman on site put them to work. About fifteen minutes later one of the bricklayers came to me at the site office and explained that they had never done any curved work and how were they to work with the line. The foreman and I spent nearly an hour explaining how this should be done. I felt sorry for the two young men, they were not to blame for this omission in their training; I blame the system.

We appear to have digressed from our line of thought on the demolition of historical architectural edifices, over the past hundred years in the Wrexham area. It is surprising to note how many of today's generation are more interested in the meaning of the two words "conservation" and "heritage" than our forefathers were.

My life as a building surveyor attached to the office of various chartered surveyors who managed the many large agricultural estates in the rural areas of North Wales and Cheshire, was a most interesting one. The variation and type of work was most gratifying, from designing and planning new buildings for the urban estates, to the maintenance and supervision of building work on the old halls and ancient farmhouses in rural areas. To meet the families who occupied the houses and the estate staff who ran them, was a rewarding occupation.

If the opportunity arises, have a look at that splendid book *"The Lost Houses of Wales"* compiled by Thomas Lloyd. It illustrates and describes some of architectural gems that have been demolished through North and South Wales.

The disappearance from the landscape of these historical buildings is a case for concern. There are a number of organisations who are trying to rescue this type of building for posterity and one of these is the Clwyd Historical Building Preservation Trust. The Trust has not long been established but is doing good work in the County. Although funds are scarce, the Trust is able to purchase derelict listed buildings to restore them to their former glory for resale. Another splendid organisation is the National Trust, who have saved many historical building throughout the country from misfortune. We are now able to visit many of their properties and enjoy their surroundings and amenities.

Those historical buildings which still stand in our area which are worthy of preservation should be taken care of; they are important to the area in which they are situated. The picturesque qualities and the harmony to the landscape or street they create are part of our heritage, let us look after them, to be handed down to future generations.

Just a note of interest with regard to the building trade; when a large building was to be erected, a body of stone-masons who were going to work on the edifice would form a Lodge on site where they would live, cook their meals and hold their meetings. In those days the various trades were a very close community, only men who had served their time in the trade would be employed on the site.

Each mason had his own distinctive mark. This was cut into the stone after he had finished working on it. These marks were of a simple design, usually about 2 inches long. The marks were kept in a register by their guild and more often than not the mark was passed on from father to son. The mark was to prove which mason had worked on any particular stone, so that the supervisor could check the workmanship and keep an account on what payment was due.

Even the carpenters had their own mark. This could be found on the various pieces of timber throughout the building. I have been able to date a building by finding the carpenter's initials cut into the purlin followed by the date when he had worked on the construction. This information could always be found at the north gable of the edifice.

ACKNOWLEDGEMENTS

The author would like to offer his grateful thanks to the staff at the County Records Office at Ruthin and Hawarden, also the staff at Wrexham Museum and the Reference Library at Wrexham, for their help while carrying out his research on the various families who occupied the houses displayed in the book.

I would also like to thank the following for their permission to use their photographs contained in the book:

Thomas Lloyd, Kilgetty: Bryn Estyn, Gardden Lodge.
P.R.Reid, Rochester: Plas Grono.
D.M.Morgan, Cardiff: Bromfield Hall.
Joan Chaloner, Wrexham: Pendine Hall.
D.Dutton, Wrexham: Grove House.
P.W.Eames, Wrexham: Plas Acton.
Information from the writings of A.N.Palmer and S.G Jarman.

Additional photographs have been supplied by the author and:
Crown Copyright: Royal Commission on the Ancient and Historical Monuments of Wales   – 811797 (Hope Hall); AA56/7860 (Broughton Hall); AA53/5596 (Bodhyfryd).
Davies Collection, National Monuments Record of Wales – 812636, 812620 (Horsley Hall); 812373 (Old Grove Park); 812654 (Gresford Lodge)
Copyright Mrs A. Littledale: from the National Monuments Record of Wales Collections   – 860736 (Gwersyllt Park)
National Library of Wales: pages 3, 8, 26 (inset), 27, 31, 32, 34, 39, 46, 59, 88
Clwyd Record Office, Hawarden: page 20
Denbighshire Record Office, Ruthin: 46, 66, 97, 98
Maelor Museum, Wrexham: 26, 44, 78

Publisher's Note

This book was found by Helen Maurice-Jones while perusing the effects of the late Raymond Lowe, during a search for photographs of the area for a forthcoming book (see back of this book). Realising its potential, agreement was reached with Lydia Lowe for the publication of her late husband's work. We are grateful to both of them for realising the worth of Raymond's book which is now being made available to a much wider audience. Mr Lowe's work seems to have been concluded; there were no partially completed entries.

The maps used herein are for identification purposes only. Some of the roads shown existed at the time of the house and may not exist now or be rights of way.

The land in the area of Acton Park was originally granted to the Valle Crucis Abbey at Llangollen by one of the chieftains of Powys. On the dissolution of the monasteries in 1536, the land was taken over by the Crown. By the year 1620 the land in Acton came into the possession of Jeffrey ap Hugh who passed it on to his son John Jeffrey, who was a Judge on the North Wales circuit. It was John Jeffrey who built the original house at Acton Park, with an area of 300 acres surrounding the hall. It was here that his grandson the notorious Judge Sir George Jeffrey was born in 1645. He was knighted in 1677 at the age of 33, and became Lord Chief Justice of England under King James II. Lord George Jeffrey of Wem died in the Tower of London in 1689 at the age of 44. He had taken up residence there for his own safety. The house was rebuilt by his nephew, Sir Griffith Jeffrey, in the late 17th century. According to the Hearth Tax Register the house was assessed as containing eleven hearths. The estate was inherited by Robert Jeffreys, son of Sir Griffith. Robert died without issue in 1714 and the property passed to his sister. Robert's brother-in-law, Phillip Egerton, occupied the hall for a number of years.

In 1747 the Acton Hall estate was sold by the Trustees of Robert Jeffreys and purchased by Ellis Yonge, the son of William Yonge of Bryn Iorcyn, Caergwrle. He carried out a remodelling scheme on the hall and died in 1785.

The Trustees then sold the estate to Sir Foster Cunliffe for £28,000 in 1786. Sir Foster was a man of literary and refined tastes and high character. He enlarged the hall in 1786-87 by adding the classical block (the right hand half of the photograph). The architect was James Wyatt and at the front elevation to this block was constructed an imposing curved stairway with a covered portico. The portico and stairway were removed and the area became a raised garden.

In 1787 Sir Foster and Lady Cunliffe established the "Society of the Royal British Bowmen", which would hold their archery contests in the grounds of the various local estates. There is an engraving by J.Townshend of one of these meets in the grounds of Erddig Hall hanging in Erddig. The entrance screen, situated at the end of the hall drive at Chester Road, was built in 1820 in stone with columns in the Doric Order. On top of the screen are four greyhounds, the crest of the Cunliffe family. The screen

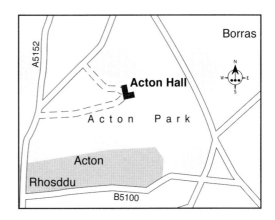

was designed by the Chester architect Thomas Harrison. When Sir Robert Cunliffe inherited Acton Hall from his father in 1834, he also carried out a major remodelling scheme to the house. He had the classical block encased in stone, and two lodges were built at the entrance to the drives. This work was carried out by the Chester architect, John Douglas.

During the First World War the hall and grounds were taken over by the Military. The Denbighshire Yoemanry was one of the regiments to be billeted there. After the war, the Acton estate was sold and purchased by Bernard Oppenheimer, a Belgian diamond merchant. In 1919, he sold about 60 acres to the Wrexham Town Council and about two years later Mr Oppenheimer sold the hall to William Aston with some of the grounds. Mr Aston opened the grounds to the public who used the grounds for recreational purposes.

During the Second World War the hall and grounds were again taken over by the Military, when the United States Army and the Indian Army were billeted there. On the area of ground the Council had bought previously, one of the largest Council Housing developments in Wales was built at Acton Park. Professor Patrick Abercrombie of the School of Architecture, Liverpool University, was commissioned to plan the layout of the estate. The foundation stone was laid in 1920 for the first group of 118 houses. William Aston later donated the hall and the grounds to the Borough Council which carried out a repair scheme on the hall, but by this time the state of the building was very dilapidated. Dry rot had set in and the cost to eradicate it was too expensive.

It was decided to demolish the classical wing in 1945 and the remainder of the building was demolished in 1956.

Thus came to an end one of the important houses in the township of Wrexham.

Bodhyfryd was built in the early 18th century in brick with stone window heads and sills. The gable ends projected above the slate roof and were finished with coping stones which were supported at the eaves by a moulded corbel. The external walls had been stucco rendered at a later date. The house was two and a half storeys in height and the plan of the building was in the shape of a 'tee'. The front elevation was symmetrical with small pane sliding sash windows. Set central of the front roof was a small dormer window with a slate roof. Under the eaves rainwater gutter was a course of dog-tooth bricks. The tall bold brick chimney stacks towered above the roof.

The house was originally built for the Dymock family of Little Acton House. William Dymock was the first to occupy the property with his wife, Elizabeth and he lived there until his death in 1764. He had given a great deal of his life to the social life of the town and had held the office of High Sheriff of the County while living at Bodhyfryd. William was the third son of John and Ellen Dymock of Little Acton House.

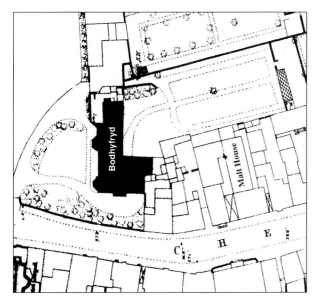

In January 1766 their daughter married Robert Wynne of Garthewin. Elizabeth was their only child and heiress to the Bodhyfryd estate. After their marriage they lived at Bodhyfryd for a period before it was leased out.

A nephew to William Dymock lived for a while at Bodhyfryd. He was followed by John Dymock who was churchwarden at the Parish Church in 1738-39. He died in June 1767, having married Elizabeth, daughter of James Morgan of Stansty, in 1756.

In 1802, Captain Thomas Lee became a tenant of Bodhyfryd. He had been a sea captain on one of the ships carrying slaves from Africa. At a later date, the property was let to a Joseph Cooper, who was the eldest son of Samuel Cooper, a timber merchant and coach builder who lived in Charles Street. On the death of Samuel in 1810, aged 62 years, Joseph took over the family business and became a wealthy merchant in the area. The area of land surrounding Bodhyfryd was in the region of nineteen acres and at the rear of the property was a cobbled yard giving access to the coach-house and stables.

In 1924 the Borough Surveyor's office was located in the house at No.1 Grosvenor Road. He shared the premises with the Health Clinic Centre but after a while the accommodation became crowded owing to the increase of work and staff at the Health Centre. It was decided to transfer the Borough Surveyor and his staff to Bodhyfryd, where they remained until after the Second World War, when they moved to the new Council Offices.

Just before the war a Major F.E.Soames lived in part of the house. During the war years the W.V.S made it their headquarters and it became a troop canteen. On the land to the rear of the building, portable sheds were erected to accommodate the Ministry administration staff. The house was demolished in April 1951.

According to the Mold and Moldsdale Chronicle there was a house on the site at Bromfield Hall in 1760. The house we are interested in was built in the early 19th century. Thomas Wightwick was mentioned in the Tithe Register as being the owner, and it is most likely that the hall was built for him; the tenant at that time was Emma Fogg.

According to the records, in 1850 the property was mentioned as Bromfield House in the occupation of William Jones, a wine and spirits merchant, trading under the name of Lloyd Jones & Co, New Street, Mold. The Bromfield Hall estate was put on the market to be sold by auction at the Albion Hotel, Chester, on the 5th August 1851, by the auctioneers, Messrs G.Churton of Chester. The area of the estate at the time of the sale was upwards of 100 acres, to be sold in 13 lots. The sale particulars of lot 7 reads: "The capital villa known as Bromfield Hall, with the usual offices, stableyard, coach-house and other buildings, all well built, the lawns, carriage drive, plantation, all walled in. The house is in the occupation of William Jones and the estate is in the township of Brincoed, in the parish of Mold, in the County of Flint."

The Bromfield Hall estate was again put on the market to be sold by auction at the Queens Head, Chester on the 21st December 1870 by the auctioneers Messrs Churton & Elplick, the whole to be sold in 7 lots. The estate at the time of the sale was in the region of six acres, the house was in the occupation of William Southall. According to the census for Broncoed township, Adam Telford was the occupier of Bromfield Hall in 1871. He lived there with his wife, Mary Jane, and their daughter, Elizabeth.

The estate again changed ownership in 1874, when William B.Marsden occupied the hall. The family was connected with the firm of W.B.Marsden, North Wales Refinery & Leeswood Vale Oil Company, Mold. Bromfield Hall was the home of the Marsden family for many years; he was the son of J.B.Marsden who was a member of the well-known solicitors in the district. There was also a brother, Frank Marsden, who was an eminent artist and would be quite often seen in the town sitting at his easel, painting.

On a business trip to London, W.B.Marsden visited an auction sale in Whitehall in passing. While at the sale he bought an old staircase for his home in Mold, and unknown to him at the time, the staircase had an interesting of history. It was discovered, after the staircase had been installed in Bromfield Hall, that it was the staircase down which the Earl of Dudley and Lady Jane Grey had walked to their execution on the scaffold. In order to install the staircase in the entrance hall, an extension to the front part of the house was necessary. The alteration to the house took place in 1874, the date being cut into the stonework over the new arch to the front entrance.

The entrance hall had a beautifully laid mosaic floor extending into the imposing porchway with its massive columns. A large dining room and drawing room led off the hall. On the first floor, the landing was used as a picture gallery and, still visible on the risers to the staircase, were seen the marks made by the Cavaliers during the reign of King Charles I.

In 1892 the property came into the ownership of David Williams, who died there in 1895. He originated from Osbourne House, Pontnewynydd, near Pontypool. He became a partner in the Alyn Tinplate Works, Maes-y-dre.

The house was then in the occupation of David Williams and on his death his son, also named David, inherited the property, but not long afterwards sold it to Frank Bright Summers who owned the Shotton Iron Works. It is believed that Mr Summers was the first person to own a motor car in Mold; this was in the year 1897.

Bromfield then came into the ownership of Peter Roberts, a native of Mold. After a successful business career in Manchester he returned to his home town. In 1911 he was elected to the office of Chairman on the Urban Council of Mold. He presented a new Town Hall situated in Earl Street. The foundation stone for the new Town Hall was laid on the Coronation Day of King George V. Peter Roberts later retired from public life and went to reside in Bournemouth where he died.

His son, Captain Norman Roberts inherited Bromfield Hall and continued his father's interest in the rubber business. Captain Roberts became a keen amateur radio ham and converted one of the rooms in the hall and set up his own amateur broadcasting station.

In 1963 Captain Roberts sold Bromfield Hall with 18 acres of land for a housing development. The hall was demolished in 1965.

BROUGHTON HALL,
PENTRE BROUGHTON, SOUTHSEA

The hall was built for the Powell family in the late 17th century. John Powell and his wife did not live very long to enjoy their new house, for in the September of 1686 his wife died and, in the December of the same year, John died. It is mentioned in the Register of St Giles Church, the Parish Church of Wrexham, that John Powell served as churchwarden in 1667-69.

Broughton Hall was not a large house. In 1670 it was assessed for the Hearth Tax as having contained three hearths. The estate was inherited by the Rev. William Powell who lived in the hall until his death in 1725. He was buried in Wrexham churchyard. He had been Rector at Llandegla Parish for a number of years.

After William Powell, the estate was inherited by Griffith Powell who resided in the hall for a short time. In 1742 another John Powell inherited the Broughton Hall estate and lived there, the estate at this time having an area of about 182 acres. The land to the estate was made up of various fields scattered in the adjoining parishes.

John Powell died in May 1749 and the interment was in Wrexham churchyard. The estate then came into the possession of Miss Anna Maria Powell, who never married. She lived in the hall and on her death the Broughton Hall estate was inherited by two sisters, Jane and Sarah Powell, in equal shares. Jane married John Jones, an attorney of Wrexham and Sarah married John Jarrett of Wrexham. There was one daughter to Sarah's marriage and five daughters to Jane's marriage. During the sisters' ownership the hall and land was let to various tenants and part of the land was sold off.

During the period round about 1835 a partnership had been formed between the Rev. John Pearce and Richard Gough who was a tobacconist in Chester. The duo began speculating by purchasing various portions of land belonging to the Broughton Hall estate, with a view to mining the minerals in the ground. Unfortunately by 1853 the partnership went into liquidation and the land in their possession was sold by auction.

In 1855 Broughton Hall estate was purchased by a syndicate comprising of the following gentlemen: Henry Robertson, William Henry Darby and his brother Charles Edward Darby. Shortly after the purchase of the land, three shafts were sunk within a short time of each other. These became Southsea Colliery, The Forge and Old Broughton Colliery.

Broughton Hall was a two and a half storey building with a slate roof. The gable ends projected above the roof and were finished with coping stones, which were supported at the eaves with moulded stone corbels. The house was built in a reddish mature coloured brick with stone features. At a later date the elevations had been stucco rendered, leaving exposed the quoins, stringer course, window-heads and sills. According to the sale particulars the accommodation comprised of: entrance

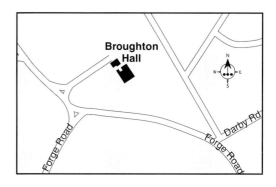

hall, dining room, sitting room, morning room, kitchen, back kitchen and pantry. The first floor was approached by a handsome carved oak staircase leading to three double bedrooms and a bathroom. On the attic floor were two double bedrooms and boxroom – daylight to these rooms in the attic was by two skylights set in the roof.

Adjacent to the hall was the home farm known as Broughton Hall Farm. The farmhouse and buildings were built in stone with slate roof. The farmyard was enclosed on two sides, the buildings comprising a shippon for 13 cows, loose boxes, engine-house, coach-house, chophouse with granary over, implement shed, pig sties and a two-bay hayshed. The farm and buildings had been left vacant for many years and became dilapidated. In 1867 the home farm had been let to a tenant by the name of Samuel Jones, who only lived there for a short time as he died twelve months after taking the tenancy, his wife having died just before her husband.

An auction was held on the farm to sell all the live and dead stock including the household effects. The sale lasted two days and was auctioned by Messrs Baugh & Jones, auctioneers of Wrexham.

What was left of the Broughton Hall estate was put on the market and sold by auction at the Wynnstay Arms Hotel, Wrexham, on the 24th April 1950 by order of the owners, The Pale and Brymbo Estate Co, Ltd. The auctioneers were Messrs A.Kent Jones & Co, Wrexham. The area of the estate at the time of the sale was in the region of 43.29 acres and the tenant in the hall at the time of the sale was Mrs M.H.Lewis, paying a rent of £30 per annum.

Part of the land was purchased by the Wrexham Council prior to the sale, on which area was built a council housing estate. During the period after the war (1939-45) the whole of the area in the region of Broughton Hall had been subject to open-cast mining, but the area was reinstated by the year 1949. Broughton Hall was demolished in 1948.

This delightful ornate dwelling was one of the largest half-timber constructed houses in Flintshire. It was built for Randall Broughton in about 1642. The infill to the timber work was in wattle and daub and the massive lateral chimney stacks were built in brick and situated each side of the house. The ornamental brick chimney stacks towered above the complex slate roof. The front projecting porch was built in stone and the family coat-of-arms was set above the heavy studded front door. This item and the two bows to the front elevation were added at a later date, sometime in the 1850s, by Robert Howard.

The early Stuart period brought about the Jacobean type of architecture, of which Broughton Hall was a fine example. The interior of the house displayed many unique timber features, demonstrating the skill of the craftsmen of those days. The house contained a number of secret staircases and hiding places for priests – relics of the more troubled religious times and the troubled political period of Charles I, the monarch who ruled despotically and made great efforts to restore Catholicism in the country.

The Howard family were benefactors to the Church of St Deiniol's in the village of Worthenbury. They gave a set of hymn and prayer books to the church together with other items. In the church is a tablet dedicated to the family who lived at Broughton Hall and it is inscribed: "In loving memory of Nugent Howard who died at Brindisi on

March 18th 1910. Regretted by his friends who erected this tablet." The tablet is now looking dilapidated and neglected.

The Broughton Hall family vault is located opposite the east end of the church. On the wall of the vault is recorded the following inscription: "Robert.H.Howard.M.A. second son of John Howard of Brereton Hall, Sandbach, died 7th October 1908, aged 81 years. Lucy Annabella, his wife, only daughter of Archdeacon Isaac Wood of Newton Hall, Middlewich. Robert Moreton, their son, Barrister at Law, died 9th January 1881. John, eldest son, died 27th March 1938, aged 85.

Although the house was a listed building, the condition of the house had deteriorated so much that it was uneconomical to have the building restored. It was demolished in 1959. It was a great loss to the Parish of Worthenbury to see such a fine building disappear from the landscape.

This was one of the most delightful houses ever to be built in the Welsh area; its loss was one of the saddest in the annals of Clwyd. It was built on an elevated site commanding one of the most beautiful and extensive views in Wales; to the south can be seen Beeston Castle, Helsby, and to the north, the Mersey and several counties in the distance.

The hall was built in stone round a brick core, the elevations were decorated on every surface with some unusual detail and the elaborate main entrance with the inscription "I.H.S. The Glory of God" was interesting. There was a house built on the site dating back to Edward ap Morgan ap Madoc, gent, of Brymbo. This original house was demolished and rebuilt and became known as Brymbo Hall. His son founded the Griffith family of Brymbo Hall in 1524. The gabled house was built for John Griffith, dated 1624, and the hall remained in the Griffith family until 1720. The hall came into the possession of Arthur Owen, who married Mary Clayton, widow of Richard Clayton, late of Brymbo Hall. Arthur Owen also had a town house in Wrexham, known as the Lodge, Bryn-y-Ffynnon Hall. It was mentioned that he had served as churchwarden at Wrexham Parish Church in 1731-32.

In the spacious garden surrounding the hall was a chapel also dated 1624, thought to be the work of the architect Inigo Jones. It is believed that the oldest part of the hall had been built by the same architect, but there is no recorded information to this effect. The original deeds to the property were burnt in a fire at Cefn Park, Abenbury, in 1794, when a great deal of information referring to the early history of Brymbo Hall was lost. In the

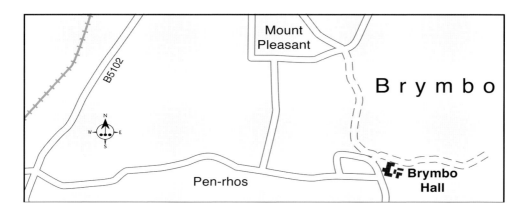

18th century a Mrs Jane Wynn lived in the hall on her own, following the death of her husband. In after years rumours were circulated about her ghost roaming the premises.

John Wilkinson purchased the estate in 1792; the area of the estate at that time was in the region of 500 acres. He was the well known Ironmaster from Bersham and the purchase price was £14,000. He borrowed £2,000 of the purchase price from two other pioneers of the Industrial Revolution, James Watt and Mathew Boulton. Before long, blast-furnaces and collieries began to appear in the parkland surrounding the hall. John Wilkinson bought additional land and extended the estate considerably during his owner-ship, and on his death in 1808, the Brymbo Hall estate was inherited by his children. The will was contested by his nephew which led to a court action and eventually the estate had to be sold to defray the legal costs. John Wilkinson, junior, lived in the hall with his two sisters (Mrs Murry and Mrs Leigh) until the property was sold.

On April 23rd and 24th, 1829, the two-day auction was held at the Wynnstay Arms Hotel, Wrexham. A detail in the sale catalogue quoted: "included in the sale is the seat or pew situated in the north aisle of Minera Parish Church, capable of holding seven people". At the time of the sale the area of the estate was about 900 acres, together with the corn-mill known as Felin Puleston, with farm and lands situated within one mile of the market town of Wrexham.

James Kyrke purchased the estate; he was the son of Richard Kirk of Gwersyllt Hill. James lived in the hall and his name is mentioned in the register of Wrexham Parish Church as having served as churchwarden in 1810-11. At a later date, James moved from Brymbo Hall to Glascoed Hall in the ffrith. Samuel Smith Adams lived at Brymbo Hall for a short time; he had connections with the Brymbo Collieries. He is also mentioned as having served as churchwarden in 1820-21. More recent occupiers of the hall were Sir Osborne Morgan, M.P. who lived there for several years, followed by Peter Williams who was works manager at Brymbo Steelworks, followed by Christmas Price Williams. The hall became vacant in 1930 and was used for housing livestock during the war years by a local farmer. It was demolished in 1973.

The original house on the site at Bryn Estyn was a small farmhouse built in half-timber construction covered with a thatch roof. At that time Bryn Estyn estate formed part of the Erlas Hall estate, Abenbury, which was owned by Roger Davies.

When William Kyffyn of Maenan Hall married Emiline, the second daughter of Roger Davies of Erlas Hall, the property known as Bryn Estyn and other properties passed into the possession of the Kyffyn family. In about 1783 Sir Thomas Kyffyn sold all his property in the Wrexham area to Richard Lloyd of Wrexham. In 1785 Richard Lloyd built a new house on the site of the old farmhouse at Bryn Estyn and took up residence there. Not long after, Sir Thomas Kyffyn moved to Bath. He died in 1814 and was buried in that city.

Richard Lloyd, in his younger days, was a wool merchant, but later in life he moved into the banking world and was the founder of two banks in the Wrexham area. During the years 1786-87 he had served as churchwarden at the Parish Church. His eldest son was born in 1783; he afterwards enlisted with the East India Company Army. Near his retirement age, he was knighted for his services. On his father's death he inherited Bryn Estyn estate and on his retirement from the East India Army with the rank of Major, Sir William Lloyd took up residence at Bryn Estyn. His son George Lloyd was born in 1815 and, when visiting Egypt in 1829, met with a fatal gun accident and died leaving no issue. Before Sir William Lloyd was knighted he held the office of High Sheriff of the County

of Denbighshire in the year 1829. He died in 1857 at the age of 75 years and was buried in the small churchyard of St Tudno on the Orme's Head, Llandudno.

Bryn Estyn estate then passed into the possession of Emily, daughter of Thomas Fitzhugh of Plas Power, Bersham. She was the wife of Captain Charles Rumley Godfrey, who died in 1893 while living at Bryn Estyn. Their son inherited the estate, but sold the property in 1903 to F.W.Soames, the brewers of Wrexham.

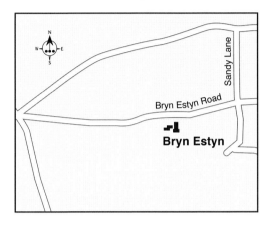

The house was built in brick with stone features and was a three storey building with slate roof. The front elevation was symmetrical with a small pediment gable over a shallow projection. Major Sir William Lloyd carried out a remodelling scheme to the house when the building was stucco rendered, and at the same time two wings were added to each end of the house.

When the Soames family purchased the property, the old house was demolished in 1903. A new, very attractive mansion was built on a new elevated site with a design of half-timber construction. F.W.Soames was elected Mayor of Wrexham in 1891 and on his death his son B.Godfrey inherited the estate from his father, who let the house on a lease to an army man by the name of General Dunn. The hall in more recent years became a school for delinquent boys.

The photograph of Bryn Estyn was kindly lent to me by Mr Thomas Lloyd, Kilgetty.

Bryn Mali (Mary's Hill) was often call Bryn Mally; this was the English version and was incorrect. The house was situated on an elevated site on the long ridge which separates Brymbo from the Moss Valley. According to the Rate Book the property was in the ownership of Thomas Brooks between the period of 1784 to 1795.

In the early 19th century the Bryn Mali estate was purchased by Richard Kirk, a leading industrialist of the Wrexham area who lived at Gwersyllt Hill. In 1840 Mr Kirk had the original house demolished and built a new house on the same site. The architect was his son-in-law, Thomas Penson of Wrexham, who had married his eldest daughter Frances. On the completion of the new house his youngest son George Kyrke took up residence and lived there for a number of years. On his father's death George and his brother James inherited the Bryn Mali Colliery and worked it in partnership from 1839. After a short period the partnership went into liquidation and the Bryn Mali estate was sold to defray expenses. George had served as churchwarden at St Giles in 1816-17.

It was from the trustees of the estate that Thomas Clayton of Chorley in Lancashire purchased Bryn Mali estate. He was a young man of 24 years when he purchased a number of collieries in the area, and became the largest employer of labour in the area. He purchased Bryn Mali in 1849 and lived there until his death in 1896. Thomas and Margery Clayton had a large family of three sons and eight daughters; they employed a large domestic staff in the house and three gardeners who looked after the large garden which surrounded the property. Margery Clayton died in the March of 1895, twelve months before her husband; Margery's name before marriage was Derbyshire.

The house was built in stone with a slate roof, there were no gables to the building and the roof was of hip construction with a parapet gutter running round the whole perimeter of the roof. The plan of the house was "L" shaped, two storeys high, with a substantial cobbled stable yard and out-buildings at the rear of the property. The ground floor comprised of sitting room, dining room, morning room, billiards room, a vinery, conservatory and the usual kitchen quarters. Upstairs on the first floor were eleven principal bedrooms, nursery and three staff bedrooms.

Below the Bryn Mali Colliery was a large pool of water with an area of about ten acres; this had been constructed by Thomas Telford for a reservoir to store

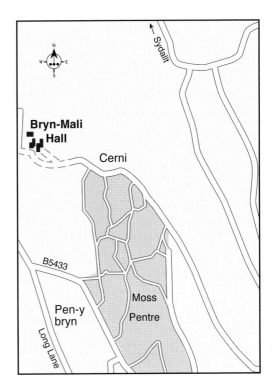

water to supply the proposed Ffrwd Canal. The canal was to have been a branch of the Ellesmere Canal. A section of the canal was excavated and can still be seen at Bithell's Lane which passes Oak Alyn to Summerhill. The canal was never completed because of the arrival of the railway system in the area.

As the years went by, Bryn Mali lost most of its former glory and the hall was let to various tenants, one of which was a family call Harris. Before the 1939-45 war the property was left vacant and it fell into disrepair, became vandalised and was demolished in 1960.

Bryn-y-Ffynnon House was the largest house in the town and was built some time in the 17th century. The whole of the building had been stucco rendered at one time, thus hiding the half-timber work which I am sure would have been a delight to see. It was a two and a half storey house with a complex slate roof profile and there were a number of large lateral chimney stacks set at each end of the building. At the rear of the house was a large cobbled yard giving access to the stables and coach-house. At one time it was suggested that the house had been built as a convent and that before the Reformation, it was used for this purpose. Certainly, the first floor rooms, where the nuns might have slept, were small and cell like, but there is no documentary evidence to confirm that the dwelling had been used as a convent.

The house had been built for the Trafford family of Esclusham Hall round about 1625, and played an important part in the social life in the township of Wrexham. The gate-house was built in brick with stone features and the centre part was two and a half storeys with two side wings of two storeys. The roof was in slate with extended gables finished with coping stones and had an interesting profile. The gate-house had been extended at a later date and was sited some distance from the house. The rooms in the house had low open-beamed ceilings, the main entertaining rooms had ornamental plaster ceilings and the floors were of stone flags. The house had been assessed for the Hearth Tax as containing 14 hearths. Over the years the house had been let to various tenants of repute. In 1670, it was let to Major John Manley. Another tenant was Colonel John Jones who was a brother-in-law to Oliver Cromwell and one of the signatories on the death warrant for King Charles I. He afterwards lost his own head when Charles II came to the throne.

When Sir Richard Lloyd was tenant at Bryn-y-Ffynnon he received King Charles there in 1642, just before the Civil War began. Between the years 1674 and 1699 the Bryn-y-Ffynnon estate came into the possession of Sir William Williams of Glascoed Hall, Nant-y-ffrith; his son adopted the surname of Wynn and became the first Sir Watkin Williams Wynn of Wynnstay, Ruabon. In 1699 we find the house was divided into three separate tenements and the gate-house divided into two tenements. Sir Henry Bunbury of Stanney in Cheshire occupied one, Lady Eyton occupied the second, and in the third lived the Rev. John Evans who turned it into a school. After his

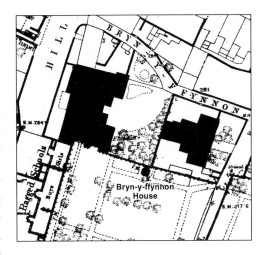

death in 1700 his widow carried on living there until 1706, when she was succeeded by Thomas Pulford.

In 1746 Sir W. W. Wynn took over the whole of the house and occupied the property. He later moved to Wynnstay Hall at Ruabon and left his brother Robert Williams to occupy the house as "Master of Bryn-y-Ffynnon House". It is mentioned in the Register at St Giles Parish Church that he served as churchwarden from 1731 to 1733 and he died in 1763 without issue. In 1751 George Warrington held the tenancy at Bryn-y-Ffynnon and lived there until his death in 1770; he was buried at Gresford, aged 75 years. He was the father of the George Warrington who became Vicar of Hope Parish in 1778.

We now come to a period when the house lost most of its former glory; the house and gate-house were let to various institutions. From 1808-18 Mr and Mrs Parry took over the tenancy of the house for a school and later the house was taken over by the three daughters of John Kenrick of Wynn Hall, Ruabon. The daughters started a school for young ladies which flourished there for ten years. In 1857 the gate-house was taken over by the Ragged School which held the tenancy for a number of years.

The first Jewish Synagogue in Wrexham rented part of the house in 1894. The other part of the house was rented by the Dissenters Chapel, under the leadership of Morgan Lloyd, for their meetings.

When the town received its Charter, the Corporation occupied the house for about 27 years until they purchased the Old Grammar School in Chester Street. Bryn-y-Ffynnon was then sold to the Shrewsbury & Chester Railway Company; it was the company's intention to build the railway station on the site of the old house, but the project did not materialise. Bryn-y-Ffynnon House was demolished in 1914 but the gate-house became a listed building and survived for a number of years. The building was let to James, James & Hatch, for their office accommodation. Eventually the gate-house was demolished to make way for a shopping development.

The original house at Bryn-y-Pys dated back to the 16th century; it was built on an elevated site overlooking the Dee valley. The estate had been in the ownership of the Price family for many generations and Nicholson's records of 1808 mentioned that: "a new mansion had been built at Bryn-y-Pys, Overton, in the county of Flint, and completed in 1807. The housewarming party for the opening of the new house had been quite an elaborate affair, there had been a masquerade and a dinner afterwards attended by the local gentry." The house was a large edifice, with an impressive dividing staircase in the entrance hall.

On the death of Francis Richard Price in 1853, the Bryn-y-Pys estate was sold; the area of the estate at that time was in the region of 2,000 acres. The purchaser was Edmund Ethelston of Uplyme Rectory in Devon and Wickstead Hall. Edmund Ethelston adopted the name of Peel in 1857.

Anne and Edmund carried out a number of alterations to the estate in the early part of their marriage. In 1881 John Douglas, the Chester architect, was commissioned to carry out a major alteration scheme to the hall. This was when the entrance tower was added to the front elevation. Three new lodges were built on the extended carriage drives to the hall, one of the drives was extended across the field to Overton Village and landscaped

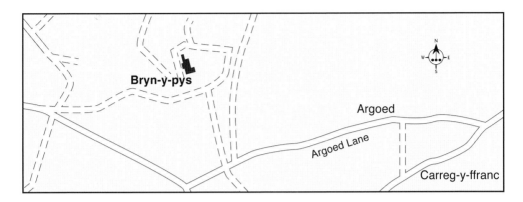

with trees and rhododendron bushes. The other drive was extended in the direction of the lower part of Maesgwaylod Hill. The more elaborate of the two entrances was the one at Overton Village, where a curved stone wall was built with tall stone gate piers and a pair of ornamental wrought iron gates.

The land agents who managed the estate were Cooke & Arkwright of Mold. The Cooke in the partnership was a relative of the Gwynsary Estate. After a short marriage Anne Peel died and Edmund later remarried a lady by the name of Anna Maria, daughter of Sir John Lethbridge. Within six years of the marriage Anna Maria died. Later Edmund Peel remarried again, this time to Henrietta Margaret, eldest daughter of Sir Hugh Williams of Bodelwydd. Unfortunately Henrietta Margaret met with a tragic accident when she was thrown from her carriage while travelling to Tedsmore Hall. After the death of Edmund, the estate was inherited by the son, who lived at the hall until his death in 1950.

The estate was then inherited by a seven-year-old relative, so the hall was let on a tenancy. At the end of this short

Front Lodge

Town Lodge

tenancy the hall stood vacant for many years. The agents were unable to find a tenant to rent the house owing to the size of the property and it was left to fall into decay. After a time the building became unsafe and in 1956 it was decided to demolish the hall and adjoining buildings.

Cefn-y-wern was originally built for the Edwards family round about the early 16th century. They were a local family and had played an important part in the social life of the district. The family were staunch Roman Catholics and refused to be otherwise. The religious changes in the Tudor period had a profound effect on the national life in the country and the Protestant Reformation was here to stay. The general climate at that time and the Tudor monarch on the throne led to the downfall of the Edwards family. By the end of the Civil War, the Edwards family were financially embarrassed and the estate was mortgaged to Richard Dutton of Chester. Although money was found to rebuild the house at Cefn-y-wern in 1620, the family only lived there until 1637. The estate was forfeited to the Crown because of their renewed allegiance to the Roman Catholic faith.

In 1662 the introduction of the Hearth Tax came about, a tax of two shillings per hearth being levied on occupiers of houses (rather than owners). It was paid in two instalments, one on Lady Day (25th March), the other at Michaelmas (29th September); Cefn-y-wern was assessed as having nine hearths.

In the late 17th century the Cefn-y-wern estate was split up, part being added to the Chirk Castle estate. When Thomas Myddelton was created a baronet in 1660, Chirk Castle was having a renovation scheme carried out, so the family vacated the castle for the duration of the work and moved to Cefn-y-wern. Thomas Myddelton died while

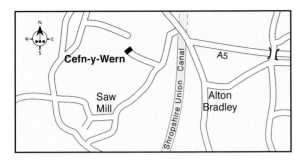

living there (the year was about 1666) but his widow Dame Mary Myddelton lived on at Cefn-y-wern until her death in 1674.

Christine, the daughter of John Edwards, married Captain Thomas Powell of Gofynys, Brymbo. In 1689, Christine made a presentation to Wrexham Parish Church of a valuable silver chalice – it is believed that the chalice dated back to the pre-Reformation period.

In 1858 Cefn-y-wern was occupied by John Dicken, a colliery owner. At a later date the house was divided into two tenements – one part of the house was occupied by John Jones, whose name is mentioned in the Register at Chirk Parish Church as having served as churchwarden in 1713-14, the other part of the house was occupied by the Rev. Thomas Smith, vicar of Chirk Parish Church.

The house was built in a random rubble limestone and at a later date the whole of the external elevations were stucco rendered. The house was a large square block with no architecturally worthy features and a number of small gables to all elevations formed a complex roof profile. The house was left vacant in the latter years and soon fell into disrepair – it was eventually demolished in 1956.

Chester Street House was a large building of renown; it was a three storey house built in brick with stone features. It was situated on the east side of Chester Street opposite the Old Grammar School. When it was first built in 1727, it was known by the local people as Mr Richards' new house, for whom the house was built.

One of the first tenants to occupy the house was Dr James Apperley, who was the grandfather of "Nimrod" Apperley, the well known sports writer in those days. After the death of Dr James Apperley in 1772, Chester Street House was purchased by John Matthews, an attorney-at-law who had his practice in the town. He lived in the house until his death in January 1807 and was buried at Wrexham. He was connected with the Matthews family at Plas Bostock, Holt. In May 1780, John Matthews married Mary, daughter of William Jones of Wrexham Fechan. John and Mary lived at Plas Bostock for a short time after their marriage, the house eventually coming into the possession of the Matthews family. There were two sons and four daughters to the marriage, but the two sons died without issue. Mary died and was buried at Wrexham in November 1828. Mary Matthews lived on at Chester Street House until the death of her son Thomas.

Chester Street House was then purchased by Thomas Taylor Griffith F.R.C.S, who lived there until his death in 1877, aged 82 years. He ran his practice from the house and was one of the eminent surgeons in the town. His son also became an eminent surgeon and, after a distinguished medical career at home and abroad, returned to Wrexham and joined his father's practice at Chester Street House. On his father's death he inherited the property and continued living there.

To the south and rear of the property was a landscaped garden, surrounded by a high brick wall. Incorporated in the garden were the stable yard and outbuildings. It is not certain when the Chester Street House was demolished, but over the years it had proved a great asset to the town, commercially and socially.

The house is shown on the 1833 edition map of Wrexham, but it is not shown on the 1872 O.S. map. The house must have been demolished within those two dates, a gap of 39 years.

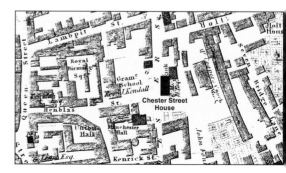

The Puleston family arrived in this country with William the Conqueror in 1066, the family first settling in Shropshire and afterwards moving to the Welsh Maelor. The estate at Emral was granted to this Anglo-Norman family in 1282. The first Sir Roger de Puleston married the daughter of the Baron of Malpas and became Sheriff of Anglesey and Constable of Caernarfon Castle. The family consisted of squire, lady and four sons for whom Emral Hall was built in the 17th century. The first part of the hall to be built was the central part, which was surrounded by an ancient moat, the east side of which was Emral Brook. The two broad and deep wings were built at a later date by Richard Tribshaw and Joseph Evans, in 1724-27 for Thomas Puleston.

In the next century after the Conquest, Robert Puleston joined the heroic Prince Owen-Glyndwr, whose sister he married. The Pulestons were fighting in the Crusade and also in the Wars of the Roses, on the side of the House of Lancaster. Roger Puleston was later elected M.P for Denbighshire in 1592 and he was knighted by King James I in 1617.

During the Civil War the family supported the Parliamentary side against the King. Judge Puleston succeeded his cousin Sir Roger Puleston to the Emral Hall estate; in 1642 the Judge died and his son, Roger Pulseton the younger, inherited the estate. He was knighted at the age of twenty but unfortunately died of a fever in 1697 and was buried, like his father, at Gresford. The estate was then inherited by a child of three named Thomas Puleston.

During the Civil War period, Emral Hall was occupied in turn by Royalists and the Roundheads. Judge Puleston's sympathies were with the Parliamentary side, which brought him into conflict with his neighbours, the Hanmers, who supported the Royalists. Sir Richard Puleston was born in 1765 and succeeded to Emral Hall estate on the death of his uncle John Puleston. He became High Sheriff of Flintshire in 1793 and was created a Baronet by King George III in 1813.

In 1840 another Sir Richard Puleston inherited Emral Hall estate and he also became Sheriff of the County. He was succeeded by his eldest son, the 3rd Baronet Richard Price Puleston, who lived most of his time in London, where he died in 1893. His half-brother, the Rev. Sir T.H. Gresley Puleston, Rector of Worthenbury, was the last Puleston of Emral Hall. It had been in their family for 700 years and was noted as one of the great houses in Wales.

Round about the 1860s, the estate was in financial difficulty, the family had left the area and were living in London. In 1895 Lady Puleston returned to the hall to carry out some restoration work after a fire at the property and by the time of her death the hall had been fully restored. The hall had two fires, one in 1895 and the other later on in 1904.

Mr & Mrs Peel Ethelston rented the hall for a time and afterwards it was rented by Mr J.W.Summers, who later purchased the property and kept it in good repair. His death signalled the end of Emral Hall. The house left vacant, it soon became dilapidated and was finally demolished in 1936. This was a sad loss to the area of such a fine example of 17th century architecture.

The hall was built in brick with stone features. On the front elevation the window heads were segmented brick arches with a stone keystone and at the rear of the house the windows had stone mullions and transom. In the old part of the house there were some fine barrel-vaulted ceilings, the plasterwork depicting the labours of Hercules between the signs of the Zodiac.

One of the barrel vaulted ceilings

Five Fords Farm formed part of the Wynnstay estate and had an area of 210 acres. John Jones had been the most recent tenant, the family first taking over the tenancy of Five Fords in 1620. The tenancy was handed down from father to son, as was typical of the Wynnstay estate, and they looked after their tenants.

The farm was situated on the perimeter of the Wrexham Industrial Estate. In the build up to the Second World War most of the farms in the area lost their land by compulsory purchase for the building of the Ordnance Factory. Five Fords was fortunate only to lose part of the land. The farmhouse was built in the early 18th century and was a two and a half storey building, a double square block with a central lead valley. The slate roof was of hip construction; at each end of the valley was an ornamental stout brick chimney stack towering above the roof. The garden to the house was small and incorporated a small orchard. The house was built to replace the ancient farmhouse which was built in half-timber construction with a thatched roof.

In 1889 part of the land at Five Fords was taken over by the Wrexham Corporation on a 99-year lease from the Wynnstay estate at an annual rent of £336, plus whatever tithe was being paid on the land. It was the intention of the Wrexham Corporation to build a new up-to-date and larger sewage plant at Five Fords. The original plant situated on land at Hafor-y-Wern had become too small and obsolete to cope with the growing and expanding population of Wrexham town.

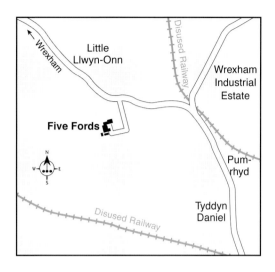

The farm house at Five Fords was demolished in 1973 and the fine old oak staircase was reinstalled in the farmhouse at Hafod-y-Bwch, Esclusham Below.

It appears that William Lee farmed part of the land at Five Fords in 1894 as tenant; he had been elected one of the members of the first Parish Council in the village of Marchwiel.

Fronheulog (Sunny Brow) was situated on an elevated site on the edge of the windswept Llandegla Moors, the altitude of the house being about 1200 feet above sea level. It had been built within the ramparts of an ancient hill fort and the remains of the trenches and embankments were still visible up to the early 19th century. The house was built of that delightful buff-coloured sandstone from the nearby local Berwig Quarry located in the Minera valley. The slate roof had a complex profile with tall ornamental stone chimney stacks towering above the steep pitch roof. The ornamental timber bargeboards to the gables added charm to the building.

Fronheulog was originally built as a hunting lodge for Thomas Edgeworth to a design by the Wrexham architect, J.R.Gummow. Thomas was the son of Thomas Edgeworth of Bryn-y-grog, Marchwiel. The house was extended and enlarged at a later date, the work being carried out in keeping with the original part of the house.

Thomas Edgeworth married Elizabeth Jane Roberts of Welshpool and became a prosperous lawyer in the town. He was descended from an old local family who had grown rich through trade and he became a leading personality in the social life of the town of Wrexham. In 1836 he carried out the duties of Clerk of the Guardians in the town and Registrar of the County Court. He was also one of the group of leaders that led a partition for the adoption of the Public Health Act, before the town received its Charter.

When Wrexham had received the Charter in 1857 Thomas Edgeworth was elected

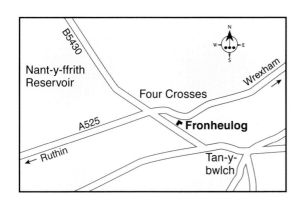

a member of the Corporation at the first election; he topped the Poll with the highest number of votes. He was elected first Mayor of the town. The first meeting of the Corporation took place in a building known as the Music Hall situated in Henblas Street. The building was later known as the newspaper office for the Wrexham Advertiser. The Music Hall was later demolished. Thomas Edgeworth died in 1869 after an active life, aged 63 years, and left two sons and two daughters.

In 1869 the Edgeworth family sold Fronheulog estate to Richard C. Kirk, who after a period of 18 years sold the property to his son Richard Venables Kyrke in 1883. The Kyrke family were speculators looking for minerals in the Denbighshire and Flintshire area.

The property was then taken over by a private girls' school. The headmistress was a lady by the name of Miss Evans. The school had previously been housed in Roseneath, a house situated in the Grove Park area of Wrexham. This house at one time had been the home of William Low, a civil engineer.

Sometime in the 1920s Fronheulog became a guesthouse and convalescent home. It became well known for the invigorating fresh air and pleasant surroundings. A number of celebrities would visit the home for their health, one of these celebrities was the actor Jack Buchanan. He suffered from a chest complaint and would often visit Fronheulog between the shows. He thought the ozone at Bwlchgwyn was like champagne.

After the closure of the home the property was taken over by the Bwlchgwyn Silica Company, who had been quarrying in the area for a number of years. The quarry workings had encroached so close to the house that it was decided to demolish the buildings; this was carried out in 1930. The site where Fronheulog had once stood has now been completely quarried out.

Just as a note of interest; Thomas Edgeworth was articled to a solicitor in Stockport on his leaving school. He sat his examinations in London, at the same time as his friend John James was taking his. John James was appointed the first Town Clerk for Wrexham Corporation.

Gardden Lodge was situated on an elevated site just below the old camp site (Y-gaer-ddin), from which the house derived its name. It is recorded that a fierce battle took place in 1167 close to the area of Y-gaer by a following of men led by Owen Cyfeiliog, a Welsh chieftain.

Gardden Lodge was built in 1799, on the boundary of the parkland belonging to Lla-nerchrugog Hall. This date with the initials R.E.J. was displayed on a stone plaque built into one of the elevations to the house. It was a three storey building built in dressed stone, with a stone moulded cornice at the eaves to the front elevation. The building had the appearance of a classical edifice and was believed to be the work of James Wyatt. A small two column portico in the Doric Order with a pediment gable graced the front entrance.

Gardden Lodge was the property of Reuben Haige of Pen-y-Gardden whose father purchased the house from Sir Henry Robertson of Pale Hall. The Robertson family came from Banff in Scotland, where he was born in 1816; the family were Presbyterians. Sir Henry was one of the great railway engineers who was responsible for the design and planning of some of the railways in the Denbighshire area.

The view from the house was not very exciting, as the vista overlooked the industrial area of Ruabon Brick Works and the Hafod Colliery. Gardden Lodge came into the possession of Edward Rowlands who held the office of High Sheriff of the County at the time he lived there. The wealthy Row-lands family were great local industrialists.

In the later years the house was left vacant and was vandalised; it was demolished in 1970. Traces of Offa's Dyke can be found close to where Gardden Lodge once stood.

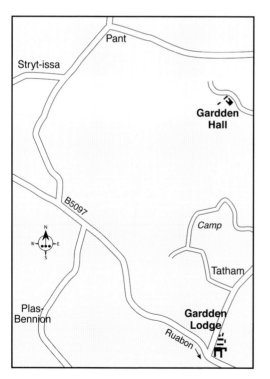

The large estate of Gredington was the seat of the Kenyon family, who were descendants of Lord Lloyd Kenyon, attorney-general in the 18th century. The house was built on the site of a medieval dwelling in 1785. It was built in dressed stone with a projecting portico to the front entrance of four columns in the Doric Order. The slate roof was of a low pitch with a parapet gutter at the eaves.

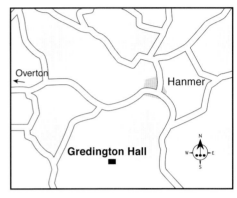

In 1810-15 the house was remodelled by the Chester architect, Thomas Harrison, when the two storey bow was built on to the front elevation. The three storey bow on the opposite side of the same elevation dates from an earlier period. The graceful small pane sliding sash windows added charm to the building. To the rear of the property an alteration scheme was carried out in the early 20th century, when columns of the Ionic Order were added to form additional accommodation.

In 1946, I was carrying out a maintenance scheme on the hall. I had some workmen renewing the leadwork to the parapet gutter on the front elevation, when dry rot was discovered in the woodwork to the gutter. On making an inspection it was found that the spores had travelled through the ceiling and floor joists on the first floor. The whole of the front wall was affected including the panelling to the ground floor rooms. When the owner received my report and cost for the eradication of the dry rot and repair to the damage, his reply to the agents who managed his estate was not good. Before he would spend that sort of money on the old house, he said, he would rather demolish it and build a new one.

The owner met strong opposition from the listed building authority, but after much paperwork and discussion the owner won his application to demolish. In about 1950 part of the building was demolished and the remainder of the house was demolished in 1982.

Left: The Lodge gates to the former hall

During the early part of the 18th century George Warrington of Bryn-y-ffynnon, Wrexham, son of John Warrington of Aigburth, Liverpool, owned a great expanse of land in the Llay area, on the outskirts of Gresford. George Warrington built a delightful circular thatched cottage on the banks of the River Alyn known as Gresford Cottage. The cottage was built as a Summer retreat for himself and family of five children.

George Warrington married Elizabeth, daughter of John Thornhill of Stanton in Der-

byshire. They lived at Bryn-y-ffynnon House, Wrexham, where he died in 1770, aged 75 years and was buried at Gresford. His widow went to live at the thatched cottage in Gresford until her death in 1788, aged 82 years. Their daughter Elizabeth married William Simpson of Hatfield in Yorkshire in 1765. Elizabeth became widowed and after a short while married John Parry of Gresford Lodge; he was M.P. for the County of Caernarvon. John Parry had built Gresford Lodge on land above the River Alyn near the thatched cottage on an elevated site. They lived at Gresford Lodge for a number of years until his death in 1797, but Elizabeth lived on at Gresford Lodge until her death in 1814. John Parry was the son of Love Parry (the elder) of Wern-fawr near Caernarvonshire, who was Attorney-General on the North Wales circuit.

Gresford Lodge was built in dressed stone to a classical design, the architect being Sir Jeffery Wyatville. The house had character and was a good example of his work. The elevation facing the river had a projecting bow with supporting columns in the Doric Order. Above, at first floor level, was a bow window capped with a lead-covered dome.

A feature on the rear elevation was a four column portico also in the Doric Order. The portico was finished with a pediment gable. The house had been extended at a later date, the work being carried out in keeping with the original design. The roof was of slate and had no gables, only hip construction, and at the eaves level was a parapet gutter round the whole of the roof.

Gresford Lodge estate was sold by auction in 1814, the area of the estate at that time being 66 acres (the old George Warrington land). Included in the sale was a farm of 50 acres known as Lyndia Farm. The estate was purchased by G. William Egerton, KCSI, who had formerly been Lieutenant-Governor of the Punjab, India. On his retirement he had lived at Coed-y-Glyn, Wrexham. William Egerton had held the post of High Sheriff of the County. He died at Gresford Lodge in 1827, but his widow Sibella lived on there for 45 years after her husband's death. She was of a dominating character and ruled the local community; she had the high stone wall built on the road boundary to the garden to have more privacy. In Gresford Church is a plaque and bust in memory of William Egerton by the well-known sculptor Sir Francis Chantrey.

After the death of Mrs Sibella Egerton in 1872 the property was sold to a number of short-stay owner-occupiers up to the beginning of the Second World War. Bartholomew Eliot George Warbarton lived for a short time with his father at Gresford Lodge; two of his books were *'The Crescent and the Cross'*, and *'Darion'*. He died at sea when the ship he was travelling on, *'Amazon'*, caught fire and sank. In the 1930s, John Woolan, the English Amateur golf champion and international player, lived at the house for a short time. Colonel Lloyd Wadle made his home there about 1939.

At the rear of the property was a cobbled yard with the usual outbuildings with coach-house and stables. Unfortunately, Gresford Lodge was situated over the coal mine workings from the nearby Llay-Main Colliery, and the house became badly affected by settlement and subsidence from the colliery workings. The property became unsafe and was demolished in 1956. The new Gresford-Pulford by-pass now runs through the Alyn Valley very close to the site where Gresford Lodge once stood.

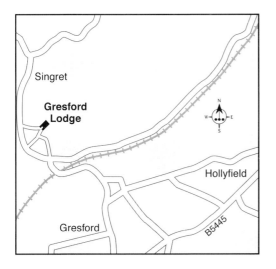

Grove House was built between 1762-65 for James Buttall who ran an iron-mongery business in The Strand in London. He purchased land in the area between Chester Street and Rhosddu Road, on which he built Grove House. The area of land surrounding the property was about 20 acres. James died in 1793 and his son Johnathan succeeded to the property. James was buried in the Dissenters' graveyard in Rhosddu Road, like his father. The field on which Grove House was built was known as Pant-y-Crydd (the shoemakers' hollow), one of the town fields.

In 1797 Mrs Ann Fryer, widow of John Fryer of Aldermanbury, London, took on the tenancy of Grove House and later purchased the property; she died there in 1817, in her 71st year. She also was buried in the Dissenters' graveyard. During her ownership of Grove House she purchased additional land, thus increasing the area to 22 acres.

After Mrs Fryer's death the property was sold and purchased by Ephraim Parkins. Grove House was then let on a tenancy to James Jackson in 1823, and he founded a private school which proved a great success. In 1841 Matthew Sobson rented the property and carried on the school. Later the it was taken over by James Parkins, a relative of the owner. In 1861 the school was taken over by G.F.Pryce Jones, who died in November 1877; after his death the school was taken over by W.J.Russell, BA.

The rear elevation of the house

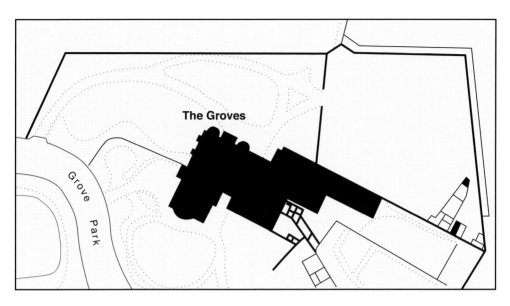

Over a period of time the school became known by various names: The Grove School, The Grove Academy, The Groves, and later it was known as Grove Park. In 1895 the school became Wrexham County School for boys. In 1915 the school formed its own OTC (officers' training corps).

Governors of Grove Park School	
Chairmen from 1893-1957	Clerks
J.E.Powell B.T.Griffith Boscawen Alderman Meredith Williams Alderman William Thomas Alderman Edward Williams	W.R.Evans J.S.Lloyd W.Emyr Williams H.R.Davies The Director of Education for the County now acts as clerk

Grove House was built in brick with stone features. The main part of the house was three storeys and the slate roof had a complicated profile. At the rear of the property were a number of two storey buildings which appear to have been added at a later date. The coach-house and stables were connected to the annex. The original Grove House was demolished in 1960.

Gwernhaylod Hall (Sunny Marsh), stood on an elevated site above the River Dee. I presume the hall derives its name from the marshy ground below the house, caused by the river flooding. The hall was surrounded by parkland and the views across the Dee were delightful.

The estate dates back to the 15th century and is probably the oldest estate in the parish of Overton, with an estimated area, at that time, of about 600 acres.

It was the abode of "Bodi", alias Madoc ap Howell, in the time of King Edward IV. The original house was demolished in 1460 and a new dwelling built on the site for Madoc ap Howell where he lived for many years. The house was remodelled about 1830, built round a 1650 core, thus suggesting that this was the fourth dwelling on the site.

Gwernhaylod was held and occupied throughout the centuries by the descendants of the Princes of North Wales, namely: Phillips, Lloyds and the Fletchers. These families inter-married with the Wynns of Gwydyr Hall, Llanrwst, and the other families of Walker and Elwes. The estate came into the possession of Colonel Phillips Lloyd Fletcher who occupied the hall for a number of years.

The estate was then inherited by Henrietta Esther Fletcher who was the last occupier of Gwernhaylod Hall; she had married the Rev. William Elwes. She was the last surviving child of Thomas Lloyd Fletcher of Maesgwaylod. After her death in 1934, Gwernhaylod estate was purchased by Hugh Peel of Bryn-y-Pys.

During the Second World War the hall and grounds were taken over by the Military to house army personnel, and the hall was badly vandalised during that period. The hall was left vacant for a number of years and became derelict; it was demolished in 1960. The stable block was left standing, although this building was in poor repair. I believe it has now been converted into a private dwelling.

Gwersyllt Hill, or Harrops Hall as it was known later by the local people, was a house of character and was situated on an elevated site above the village of Gwersyllt. It was built in dressed sandstone with moulded stone mullions and transom windows; above the window heads were moulded drip beads. The decorated gables projected above the slate roof. Part of the house was in two storeys, the other part was in three. The tower was four storeys and was capped with a bulbous dome. Later, after the hall came into the possession of a local architect, it was enlarged.

The hall was built for an industrialist by the name of Richard Kirk, who moved to the Wrexham area in 1775 from Chapel-en-le-Frith in Derbyshire; his wife was Ellen Venables. They had five sons by the marriage; the two eldest never married and died without issue. The other three sons were James Kyrke, who was born in 1780, lived at Brymbo Hall and Glascoed Hall in Nant-y-ffrith and died in 1857; George Kyrke, who was born in 1780, lived at Bryn Mali, Brymbo, and died in 1858; and Richard Venables Kyrke, who was born in 1787 and died in 1868. The sons used a variation to the family name which was carried on by their descendants. The family were staunch members of the Chester Street Presbyterian Chapel. The Kirk family name crops up frequently in connection with other properties in this book.

Richard Kirk did not take up residence at Gwersyllt Hill until later on in his life; the property was let to various tenants. On his death in 1839, aged 91 years, the Gwersyllt Hill estate was bequeathed to his daughter Frances and her husband, Thomas Penson, a

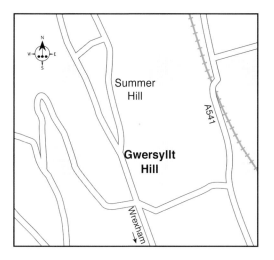

member of a local family of architects.

Thomas Penson and his family took up residence at Gwersyllt Hill in 1841 after he had carried out a remodelling scheme on the property, at the same time enlarging the size of the hall. At one time the house was covered in ivy creeper, but this was removed during the renovation. At one time the house was known by the local people as Harrops Hall, named after one of the tenants who held a lease on the property.

In the early 1950s the property was purchased by a syndicate who opened it up as a social club (Summerhill Social Club); this venture did not last very long. Sometime in the 1970s the property was taken over for a night club, but failed as a commercial enterprise. After the night club closed down, the property became dilapidated and the hall and the stable yard buildings were demolished in 1982.

The greater part of Gwersyllt was owned by one of the great Welsh clans; in later years the members of the clan adopted the name of Sutton and Lewis. The Sutton family took their name from Sutton Isycoed, an area on the south-east side of Wrexham, where the family held land and property. This had been bestowed on them by an ancestor, Morgan ap David ap Goronwy ap Madoc, Lord of Sutton Isycoed dating back to 1416.

At the end of the 16th century there were three large estates in Gwersyllt belonging to three Welsh families, Shakerley, Robinson, and Cawley. The Shakerley family lived at Gwersyllt Issa which later became known as Gwersyllt Mill.

In 1620 Gwersyllt Issa was held by William Lewis; his share of the estate was one third, with John Sutton senior and John Sutton junior holding two thirds. The area of the estate at this time was in the region of 326 acres. In 1660 Captain Ellis Sutton sold the Gwersyllt Issa estate to Colonel Sir Geoffrey Shakerley. At the time he was living there in 1684, the house was assessed as containing ten hearths for the Hearth Tax. John Sutton senior died in February 1625 and his son John Sutton junior died just seven days later.

Capt. Ellis Sutton fought on the side of the King during the Civil War, but unfortunately for the family, it was the losing side. The family lost their estate and were fined £57 by Parliament, this figure being one sixth of the value of the estate. Although he lost his estate to the Crown, he was still in favour with the authorities, because he was appointed Captain of the local militia during the reign of King James II.

On his father's death in 1713, George Shakerley came into possession of Gwersyllt Issa. Mrs Ann Williams of Stansty Isaf, who died in May 1716, was the widow of Robert Williams; she bequeathed all her lands and tenements to George Shakerley of Gwersyllt Issa. Stansty Isaf afterwards became part of the Erddig estate. This was when he sold Gwersyllt Issa and went to live at Acton. Gwersyllt Issa eventually became part of the Wynnstay estate. This came about when Sir Geoffrey Shakerley died in 1697; he was buried in Nether Peover Churchyard in Cheshire. His eldest son, George Shakerley, married Anne, youngest daughter of Sir Walter Bagot of Blithfield, Staffordshire. There were ten children to the marriage. He died in February 1726 aged 73 years and was buried in the same place as his father. His second son, Peter, inherited Gwersyllt Issa and lived there until his death in 1781, leaving one daughter Eliza, who married Charles Buckworth. Charles was a descendant of the Shakerley family of Somerford Park. Frances, the only married sister of Peter Shakerley, became the second wife of Sir Watkin Williams Wynne, the third Baronet. Through their marriage Gwersyllt Issa became part of the Wynnstay estate.

In April 1738 Gwersyllt Issa was burnt to the ground. The old hall was destroyed but the stables and outbuildings survived the fire. A new house was built on the site in the style of a farmhouse.

Gwersyllt Uchaf together with Gwersyllt Park and Gwersyllt Issa was one of the great estates in the parish of Gwersyllt. They were all originally in the same ownership (see Gwersyllt Issa); later the members adopted the surname of Lewis and Sutton. They were part of the Sutton family from Sutton Isycoed.

The only description of the house on the estate was that it was a large rugged type of farmhouse built in stone with a slate roof. The plan of the building was that of a medieval open hall, the large room open to the apex of the roof with two storey accommodation at both ends of the hall. The large room was entered from a passage that ran across the building. The land attached to the estate at that time was in the region of 258 acres.

Gwersyllt Uchaf was first mentioned in 1620, when it was in the occupation of William and James Lewis who were members of the Sutton family of Isycoed. In 1670 the estate came into the possession of Robert Cawley. How he came to be in possession of the property is not quite clear. In 1682 Robert Cawley married Sarah, daughter of one of the Brettons of Shrewsbury; they married at Gresford Church. There were four children to the marriage, James, Robert, Sarah and Margaret.

James inherited Gwersyllt Uchaf after his father's death in 1688. James died in April 1712 at the early age of 28 and his brother Robert died in infancy the following July. Sarah also died in infancy when she was 9 months old. Margaret was the only one of the family to survive and she inherited the estate. On the death of James, the male line of the Cawley family died out.

Margaret Cawley married Thomas Humberston of Croes Iocyn, Holt, in 1707 in St Giles Church, Wrexham. Their eldest son Cawley, later Cawley Humberston-Cawley of Gwersyllt Uchaf, married Anne, second daughter of John Robinson of Gwersyllt Park in May 1731. Their son John Humberston-Cawley married Mary, daughter of Charles Floyer, of Hints Hall in Staffordshire, and sister to Ralph Floyer, who died unmarried; thus Mary became heiress to the Hints Hall estate. Anne Robinson became the heiress of the Gwersyllt Park estate in 1733, but she sold it rather than passing it onto her son. In April 1775, the latter purchased Gwersyllt Park.

In April 1775, the area of the estate was 450 acres. In 1805 he sold it to John Atherton of Liverpool.

Thus, the two estates, Gwersyllt Uchaf and Gwersyllt Park became one estate. What happened to the house on Gwersyllt Uchaf was uncertain, as there was no mention of the house after the Cawley family ceased to live there.

Gwersyllt Park was one of the three great estates in the Gwersyllt area. It dated back to 1563, when it was in the possession of John ap John Lewis and was also known as Middle Gwersyllt. The estate was originally owned by the Lewis and Sutton family. The house and buildings were surrounded by 84 acres of parkland on an elevated site overlooking the River Alyn.

Edward Lewis, a member of the Welsh clan who held the estate with the Sutton family, (the two families had adopted the surname of Lewis and Sutton) sold Gwersyllt Park to Nicolas Robinson, Bishop of Bangor. On his death in 1620, his eldest son inherited the estate, which at that time had an area of 199 acres of land. This son was named William Robinson. He lived for a short time at Gwersyllt Park with his wife Jane, daughter of Edward Price of Newtown in Montgomeryshire, and there were three children to the marriage. On William's death his second son, Colonel John Robinson, inherited the estate. He had married Margaret, daughter of Colonel Edward Norris of Speke Hall, Lancashire. Col. John Robinson was Companion-at-Arms with Col. Geoffrey Shakerley of Gwersyllt Issa.

During the Civil War, Col. John Robinson supported the Royalists. At one time in the war he was involved in a skirmish with a party of Roundheads and he was taken prisoner. He managed to escape his captors who were intending to hang him from the oak tree in front of his house. He was able to escape to France where he lived until the Civil War had finished. On his return to this country in 1645, after twelve years in exile, he found his estate had been confiscated during his absence by Parliament and was occupied by a person who had fought for the Parliamentary cause. Col. John Robinson had his estate restored to him by King Charles II, having been able to purchase it back from the Treason Trustees with help from his uncle Piers Robinson. On his death in 1681, aged 65

years, Col. John Robinson was buried at Gresford and the estate was inherited by his eldest son, William. He married Anne, daughter and heiress of Timothy Myddelton of Pant Iocyn, Gresford, in 1682.

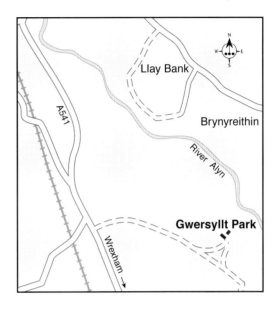

On William's death, his eldest son John inherited Gwersyllt Park in 1717. He had married Elizabeth, daughter of Sir Griffith Jeffreys, of Acton Hall. When their eldest son inherited the estate, he was the last in the line of the Robinsons. William died in 1733 when he drowned off the Skerries in a shipwreck.

Gwersyllt Park was purchased by Edward Lloyd in 1763, the area of the estate at this time being 450 acres. In 1775 the estate was sold to John Humberston-Cawley, who in 1805 sold Gwersyllt Park to John Atherton of Liverpool.

John Williams bought the estate from John Atherton and lived there for many years. He was the second son of Thomas Williams, the well known attorney of Llanidan, Anglesey, and was the founder of the Williams Bank at Chester and Bangor. His father owned the Parys Copper Mine in Anglesey. He married Elizabeth, daughter of Dr Currie of Broughton near Chester. He died without issue in 1848, aged 60 years. His widow lived on at Gwersyllt Park until her death in 1855, aged 72 years. The estate then passed to his nephew Colonel M.J.Wheatley.

Coal mining in the area was extensive and unfortunately the house was situated over some of these mine workings. The house became affected by subsidence and cracks appeared in the walls and ceilings. The building became unsafe to live in and was demolished in 1910.

Hafod-y-wern was a delightful half-timber constructed house built in 1611 for Hwfa-ap-Iorworth, the last owner of the estate in the direct line of the Welsh family Hywel of Goronwy. There were two daughters to his marriage of whom Alswn (Alice), as the eldest, inherited the estate. She married Hywel-ap-Griffith of Bersham; there was one daughter to the marriage, who married John Puleston of Berse (now known as Upper Berse Farm). Hafod-y-wern estate remained in the possession of the Puleston family but they ceased to live there after 1757. The property was let to the first tenant, Edward Roberts, who farmed there.

John Puleston served as church-warden at the Parish Church in 1643-1644; he was married to Eleanor, daughter of Sir Kenrick Eyton of Eyton Isaf. John, the son of Robert and Jane Puleston, was appointed to High Sheriff of the County. It was also mentioned that Edward Roberts of Hafod-y-wern served as churchwarden at the Parish Church in 1755-56; he died at Hafod-y-wern in 1780.

In 1869 Hafod-y-wern estate came into the possession of P.D.Davies Cooke, who had been the estate agent for the Puleston family for many years. In 1869 Hafod-y-wern was let on a lease to the Wrexham Corporation for the sewage farm to cope with the new drainage scheme from the town. Hafod-y-wern at that time was 84 acres and appeared an ideal site for the sewage works. The Corporation lease on the farm was for twenty-one years; the plant was designed by one of

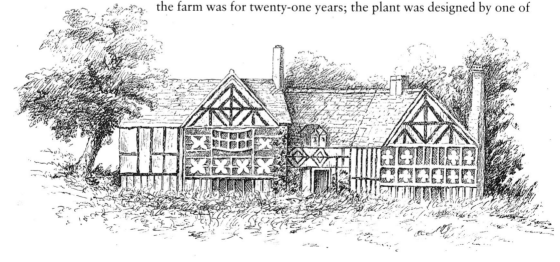

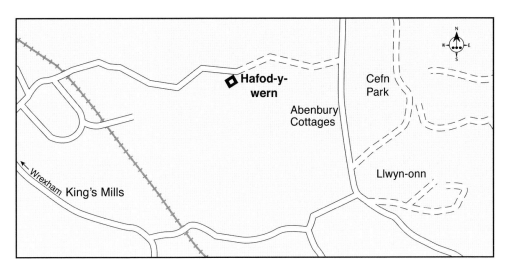

the leading sanitary engineers of the day, Robert Rawlinson, at a cost of £10,450.

The sewage plant was operated by the Corporation for about two years, but it was found that the running of the plant was too costly and was inefficient. In 1872 the plant and works were leased to a Colonel Alfred.S.Jones VC who was an experienced engineer in that field. The rent the Colonel paid for the plant was £350 per annum. Under his enterprise and control the plant prospered and was successful.

By the year 1889 the population of Wrexham Town had rapidly increased and the sewage plant at Hafod-y-wern had become too small to cope with the increase. It was decided by the Corporation to resite the plant at Five Fords Farm in Marchwiel; this which was a much larger site. When all the activity was transferred to Five Fords the plant at Hafod-y-wern was closed down.

The old house at Hafod-y-wern was reduced in size in 1829, the part on the left-hand side being demolished. This part of the house contained the great hall which at one end accommodated the dais or low platform where the Lord of the Manor sat with his family; the walls to the hall were clad with wainscot panelling. On the side of the house was a lateral chimney stack, built in stone, towering above the slate roof.

Opposite page: Drawing by Lady H.C.Cooke. From the writings of A.N.Palmer

The Henblas (Old Hall) was a large house situated on the south side of Henblas Street, at the end of a long garden stretching down to Queen's Street. The house was built in the early 18th century in brick with stone features and was a three storey building with a slate roof. The entrance gave access to the street and, with a two column portico in Ionic order, gave distinction to the front entrance. To the front of the house was a narrow forecourt fenced off with iron railings set on a stone plinth. The house had stone quoins at the corners of the building and the heavy decorative eaves added a certain amount of charm to the house.

Henblas Street in those days was a straight cobbled street leading to Chester Street.

When the Grammar School and the Congregational Chapel were built, that part of the street between the two buildings was reduced to a narrow passage. The street, as we know it today, developed into the sweeping curves at a later date. To the side of the house were the stable and coach-house buildings surrounding a cobbled yard. Entrance to the yard was by a pair of iron gates.

In 1780 The Henblas and the Rainbow Inn, situated in Queen's Street, were all part of an estate that was owned by the Rev. John Jones, and they remained in his ownership for about twenty years. He had been Rector of Knocking Parish in Salop from 1761 to 1798. He had also been Vicar of Llansantffraid-yr-Machain from 1783 to 1798 and he had family connections with the Jones family who lived at and owned Coed-y-Glyn, Wrexham.

The first tenant to occupy The Henblas was an apothecary by the name of John Myddelton, whose father was also an apothecary who lived at 34, High Street, Wrexham. John

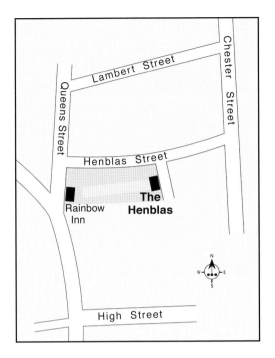

lived at The Henblas from about 1748 until his death in October 1761. He had family connections with the Myddelton family who lived at Gwaunynog.

John Myddelton was succeeded at The Henblas by Miss Anne Maria Powell in 1764. She was the last in line of the Powell family of Broughton Hall, Southsea. Before moving to The Henblas, Miss Powell had been living at Plas Gwern in Tuttle Street, Wrexham. According to the Rate Book she was still living at The Henblas in 1771 and she died there in 1778.

The next tenant to be mentioned was John Jones who kept the stationer's shop in the town. It was not long after this last tenant to live at The Henblas that the building was demolished round about 1808, and three detached houses were built on the site. Also a large building called The Birmingham Square was erected on part of the garden. Access to the building was by a steep passage from the Rainbow Inn in Queen's Street. This was a building used by the travelling traders to sell their wares and was later converted into the Vegetable Market.

This attractive house of a classical design was a two and a half storey building. It was built in 1740 on an elevated site above the village, in a hand-made brick of a reddish mature colour with stone features. The stone quoins, stringer course and keystones to the window heads stood out in bold feature. The arch to the window heads were of splayed bricks, the sliding sash windows being typical of the period. The symmetrical design to the front elevation and the proportions of its various parts suggests the plan and design had been carried out by one of the leading architects in the area. The high ceilings, the moulded cornice and the ornamental plasterwork to the internal rooms added to the pleasure of living in this type of house. Sash windows were introduced to London after the Great Fire of 1666. They were first used outside London at Chatsworth House in c.1676 and soon became very popular. However, by the 1740s the glazing bars had become much more slender.

The imposing front elevation had two shallow projecting wings, the bold feature of the front entrance with its moulded stone surround and pediment head adding grace to the entrance. The low pitched roof with the wide overhanging eaves gave the building a definite roof line. The brick chimney stacks sat symmetrical of the ridge line. The roof had no gables, only hip construction.

The house was built for George Hope, who had married Elizabeth Charlotte, daughter of Sir Thomas Longueville of Esclus Hall, later called Esclusham Hall, at Rhos-tyl-len. He came to Hope Parish after he had severed his connections with the Broughton and Bretton Parish, owing to financial reasons. The hall was built on the site of an old farmhouse and buildings, which his family had held since the reign of King Henry VI (1422-61). In his latter years at Hope Hall he was joined by his son-in-law, the Rev. John Ryton, who had married Penelope Grey, the daughter of

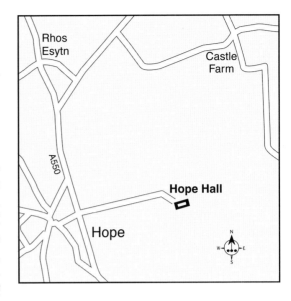

George Hope. John and Penelope had a large family; their children's names are recorded in the Parish Register at Hope Church where they were baptised. John Eyton was related to the Eyton family who lived at Leeswood Hall.

Hope Hall estate had been farmed by various tenants in more recent years, the last occupants of the hall being Mr & Mrs Thomas Cadwaladr. Thomas was better known as 'Tom the dealer'. He was born at the Four Crosses Inn, Bwlchgwyn on the edge of the Llandegla Moors. His mother inherited the inn from her grandfather when she was quite a young woman. His father was Cadwelyn Cadwaladr who was a stonemason and died at a young age. Tom had become quite a character among the farming community with his dealing with livestock and was held in high esteem.

Hope Hall was demolished in 1960; it was surprising to see the house disappear from the landscape because the structure was in good condition.

Plas-yn-Horsli or Horsley in the Parish of Gresford, the Lordship of Merffordd and the Principality of Powys Fadog, was, at the Domesday Survey, a possession of the Church of St.Werburgh in Chester. The Norman surveyors called it Odeslie and recorded the area as one "carucate", formerly as much land as one team of oxen could plough in a year, about 240 acres, worth three shillings. In 1272 Horsley and its mill were in the occupation of one Urien de Sancto Petro, who held the freehold by the service of providing ten conservators of the peace, whose "Habiliments" were paid for by the City of Chester at the rate of thirty shillings a year. Powisland in the Marches was debatable territory and no doubt needed close watch and a patrol at all seasons.

By 1371 Jeuan ap David ap Magod, son of David hen of Burton and Llai, had come into possession of Horsley. His daughter and heiress, Anharad, married Jeuan Lloyd of Trefalun (Trevalyn), and their daughter Margaret brought the estate as her dowry to Howell ap David ap Gruffyd Fychan whose descendants, the Powells were to remain in possession for several centuries. Between 1530 and 1550 Thomas Powell, son and heir of Powell ap David, and Margaret his wife, built Horsley Hall on the site of an older dwelling house. This was one of the large half-timbered and plaster houses so much in fashion in that part of the County in those days. It was built on the slope of Marford Hill with beautiful views over the River Dee and Holt Bridge.

A minute description of the estate is given in 'Nordens of Bromfield and Yale' (1620). Attached to the mansion house was the Dovecote Croft and horse pasture or Horse Ley; there were extensive freehold and leasehold lands and messuages (a dwelling house with the adjacent buildings) in Allington, Gresford and Burton. Here he was succeeded by his

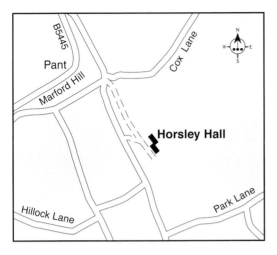

son Sir Thomas Powell and grandson, who was High Sheriff of Denbighshire in 1616, and then by the Royalist Sir Thomas Powell, first baronet. Horsley continued in the eldest branch of the Powell family until the extinction of the male line in 1707, when it descended to the children of Winifred Lloyd, sister of the last baronet, Sir Samuel Powell. Edward Lloyd owned the estate when he was Mayor of Holt in 1740.

About 1792 the estate passed by purchase to John Hughes of Wrexham whose son there kept his position of Deputy Lieutenant and High Sheriff of the County. The property was sold by his widow to two purchasers, one of whom was Frederick Potts, a solicitor of Manchester, who was also agent to the Duke of Westminster. Frederick Potts demolished a greater part of the old moated hall and rebuilt it. After his death in 1898 his son sold the estate to Mr Alfred Ashworth who was residing there in 1905. In 1917 the estate was purchased by Lord Wavertree who improved the gardens. The estate was sold by auction in 1933 to a demolition contractor, but it survived until 1963 when the house was eventually demolished. In the Second World War the property was taken over by the Army.

Between the late 17th century and the middle of the 18th century, the area of ground on the banks of the River Gwenfro and north of Pentre'r Felin Bridge was known as the Walks and Ireland Green. At that time there was no dwelling on the Ireland Green site, only a barn and a meadow in the ownership of Edward Jones, a tanner, where he grazed his cattle. It is recorded in the Register at St Giles Parish Church that he had served as churchwarden in 1670-71, and again in 1682-83.

It was not until 1762 that mention is made of a dwelling house being built on the Ireland Green site; this would most likely have been a half-timber structure with a thatch roof. The land was then in the ownership of Edward Tomkies who owned one of the tanneries in the Pentre'r Felin area. He was the son of John Tomkies who also owned his own tannery in the area. Edward's name is also recorded as having served as churchwarden at St Giles Church in 1751-52. Edward died at Ireland Green in 1779 and was buried at Wrexham. About four years after his death, the Ireland Green property passed into the possession of William Edwards who owned a tannery in Pen-y-bryn. His son Watkin Edwards, who was in the business with his father, also lived at Ireland Green, but he died young, aged 37 years, in September 1819.

In 1844 the Ireland Green estate passed into the ownership of John Bennion, a wealthy lawyer of an ancient local family. Bennion Road in the town was named after the family. He rebuilt the house at Ireland Green in an early Victorian style; the front elevation was clad in dressed stone while the remainder of the dwelling was built in brick. The plan of the building was a double block with a central lead valley. On the east corner to the front elevation was a square bay window built in stone with sliding sash windows. At the same time the spacious gardens surrounding the house were landscaped and part of the River Gwenfro that ran through the garden was piped

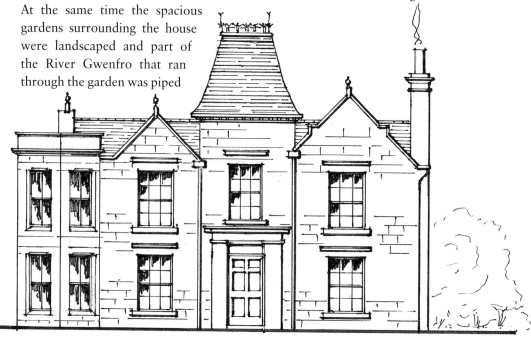

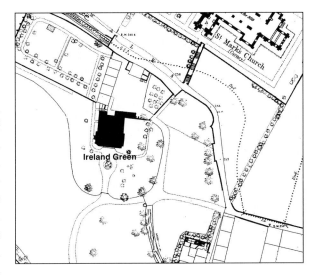

Ireland Green

underground. It was said that the lawns, borders and paths were quite a show. The large mature orchard stretched as far as the garden belonging to Bryn-y-ffynnon House. John Bennion married Hannah, daughter of William Rowe of Sibbesfield in Cheshire. They lived at Ireland Green until John died in September 1850; the area of the estate during his time was in the region of four and a half acres. By the middle of the 19th century a brewery had been built within the curtilage of the property and became known as Ireland Green Brewery.

By the end of the 19th century the area around Ireland Green and the Walks had become very industrialised. The Ireland Green estate had sadly fallen from its former glory; the area had become noted for the many tanneries, skinyards and curries that had sprung up in a very short time. The property of Ireland Green had become a little oasis midst the squalour of this industrial part of Wrexham. In more recent years, this area has seen great changes; the site has now been developed into a modern shopping centre with spacious car parking.

Note: 19th century OS Maps refer to the house as Island Green.

There is no mention of this estate before the year 1692, when John Dymock was already living at Little Acton. The only recorded history of the Dymock family starts with John Dymock, whose death is mentioned in 1706, when he was buried in Marchwiel graveyard. He had married Ellen, daughter of Thomas Puleston of Pickhill Hall, Sesswick. There were five children to the marriage; John the eldest, inherited Little Acton on the death of his father. He married Jane Jennings of the Parish of Marchwiel; there was only one son to the marriage and he was also called John. At a young age he married Elizabeth, daughter of James Morgan of Stansty. This John was born in 1723 and died in 1738. This branch of the Dymock family was connected with the Dymocks of Bodhyfryd, Chester Street, also of Sontley and Pen-Lan.

Sometime between 1732 and 1742 the Dymock family ceased to live at Little Acton. The estate was let on a tenancy in 1772 to The Rev. George Warrington and in 1796 the tenancy was held by John Hughes. It was in 1792 that John Hughes purchased some land adjoining Little Acton from the Horsley estate in the parish of Gresford. John Hughes was succeeded as tenant of Little Acton by his son, Doctor Francis James Hughes, who in 1854, held the office of High Sheriff of the County of Denbighshire. He later held the office of Chairman of the Bench of Magistrates and in 1762 he held the office

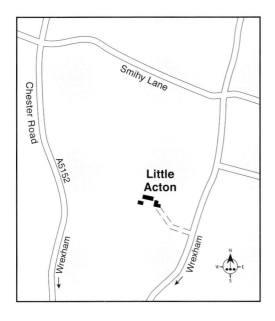

of Mayor of Holt.

For many years the old octagonal font had gone missing from the parish church of Gresford. It came to light in the garden of Little Acton, where it was being used as a flower basin. The font was restored to the parish church by Dr F.J.Hughes in 1842. The Doctor died at Little Acton in 1856, aged 68 years.

With the death of Doctor Hughes, the male line of the Dymock family died out. All the Dymock estates passed to Robert Wynne by marriage; he had married Elizabeth, only daughter and heiress of William Dymock of Bodhyfryd. It was in 1882 that the Wynne family of Garthwin sold Little Acton estate for the sum of £9,000 to Sir Robert A.Cunliffe; the area of the estate at that time was in the region of 80 acres.

The house at Little Acton was built in brick with stone features; it was a double square block with central lead valley. There were bold brick chimney stacks at the gable ends towering above the slate roof. To the front elevation were three small gables and the building was a two and a half storey edifice of great charm. Very little of the house was visible because of the mass of creeper covering the walls. Only the outline of the windows could be seen.

Little Acton Hall was demolished sometime in the middle of the 20th century to make way for a housing development.

During the late 17th century, when Llay formed part of the huge ecclesiastical parish of Gresford, there were three estates of note in the Llay area. On the estates were large houses after which the estates were known, the largest being Llay Hall which was assessed for the Hearth Tax as having ten hearths. Next came Apothecary's Hall named after the owner Richard Jones who was an Apothecary in Wrexham; this estate later became known as Acre Hall. This house was also assessed for the tax as having seven hearths. The original house at Llay Place was of half-timber construction and was assessed as having five hearths; this estate was in the ownership of Robert Murray.

During the early part of the 19th century Richard Kirk, his wife and purchased Llay Place estate and took up residence there. The family were speculators in minerals in

the Wrexham area; they came to Llay in search of coal. The family was in the habit of purchasing small estates if he thought there was the likelihood of finding minerals in the ground. They would demolish the old house and build a new house on the same site; this is what he did at Llay Place. They had the old house demolished and built the new dwelling there in 1865.

Richard Kirk's son-in-law, Thomas Penson, was the architect for the new house. The structure was a good example of his work. The low pitched roof, the symmetrical elevations and the tower with the pavilion roof, the top of which was finished with a wrought iron finial to the top of the tower were typical of his design. There were later additions carried out to the house at various times. To the rear of the property was a the cobbled courtyard which gave access to the stables and coach-house. The spacious garden that surrounded the house was laid out with mature trees and shrubberies of rhododendrons,

in addition to which was an expanse of parkland. Running through the grounds was a small stream known as "Nant-y-gaer Brook", sometimes called "Black Brook". It is believed that the source of the stream is from a spring located under the slag bank on the site of the disused Llay Main Colliery. The stream is a tributary of the River Alyn.

On the 18th of October 1906, the surveyor appointed by the Llay Main Colliery ordered a borehole to be made in the parkland to Llay Place, with the objective of proving the coal-seam and the depth under that area. It was not until the 14th of September 1908 that the main coal-seam was proved at a depth of 2,373 feet at that borehole.

The house at Llay Place had seen many changes during its 134 years of existence and many families had made it their home. After its original use as a private dwelling, it was later converted into flats. In the 1920s the house was rented by the Miners' Welfare for their Institute until a new building was completed. The building of this was started in 1929 and opened in 1931. A boys' school took over the property and was there for a number of years. During the war years (1939-45) the house and grounds were commandeered by the military to house American troops. After the war the house was divided into two dwellings to accommodate two families.

As time went by the property was left vacant. It was difficult to find a tenant to occupy the property and eventually the house became dilapidated. In 1999 the house and grounds were sold to developers. They were demolished in that year and a small domestic development sprang up where once stood a noble edifice.

The property known as Yspytty Uchaf was approached by a curved drive leading from Chester Road; the tradesmen's entrance gave access from Rhosddu Road. The original house on the site was an old farmhouse built in half-timber construction with a thatched roof. It was a smallholding dating back to the 16th century. The land was scattered about the area, but most of the fields were situated behind the property in Lambpit Street. The old farmhouse was demolished in the late 17th century and a large new house built on the site. The large garden that surrounded the house was laid out with orchard, mature trees and shrubs and a stone wall was built on the boundary giving the house privacy.

The central part of the house had three storeys; the two side wings were only two storeys. The house was built in brick with stone features and set central to the front elevation was a four column portico in the Doric Order providing a balanced symmetrical elevation with tall sliding sash windows. The tall brick chimney stacks towered above the slate roof.

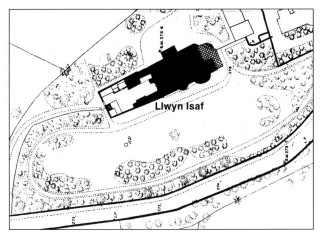

In 1759, or around that period, Sir Thomas Longueville rented the property as his town house, but, after living there for a short time, he died at Yspytty Uchaf in 1760. His main place of residence was Esclus Hall, Rhostyllen.

In 1699 the Rate book recorded that Yspytty Uchaf was in the occupation of Robert and Godfrey Lloyd, who were connected with the property up to the year 1720. Godfrey was the son of Robert Lloyd and it is suggested that it was this family who built the new house at Yspytty Uchaf.

After the tenancy of Sir Thomas Longueville, the property was taken over by Rev. John Salusbury for a short time. A lady by the name of Mrs Wynne took over the tenancy with the adjoining croft.

In 1765 George Ravenscroft occupied Yspytty Uchaf and remained there until his death, the date of which is rather obscure but might be around 1782. His widow lived on at Yspytty Uchaf until her death; it appeared that George Ravenscroft had purchased the estate before his death. He had married Elizabeth, daughter of John Puleston of Pickhill Hall and their marriage was blessed with a large family.

Yspytty Uchaf was purchased in 1826 by Canon George Cunliffe when he was offered the incumbency of St Giles Church, Wrexham. He was the son of Sir Foster Cunliffe of Acton Hall. It was at this time that the name of the house was changed to Llwyn Isaf. When George retired from the incumbency in 1876, he donated Llwyn Isaf to the parish of Wrexham to be used as the vicarage for St Giles Parish Church. George Cunliffe went to reside at another of his properties on the outskirts of the town where he eventually died.

The Llwyn Isaf estate was purchased by the Wrexham Council in 1953, when it was used for office accommodation by the Council. Later the house and buildings were demolished to make way for the new Council building for office accommodation.

Minera Hall was built in 1800 for Robert Burton who was a speculator and prospector for minerals in the Wrexham area. He was a shareholder in the local lead mines and also had an interest in some coalmines in the area. Robert Burton had lived at Bryn Mefus (Strawberry Hill) before he moved to Minera; he had served as churchwarden at St Giles Parish Church, Wrexham in 1819. He died at Minera Hall in March 1819, aged 74 years. His son John Burton inherited Minera Hall and married Elizabeth, one of the

daughters of Richard Kirk of Gwersyllt Hill. His wife Elizabeth died in 1829, aged 43 years and John died in 1860 aged 79 years. Their son, the Rev. Robert Owen Burton M.A, inherited the hall and estate from his father. He had married Jane Wynn, the second daughter of the Rev. Rowland Williams, Rector of Ysceifiog. Robert presented to the Parish Church of Minera the stained glass east window in memory of his father and mother; it was the work of A.Gibbs of London. There were two sons to the marriage, John Robert Burton who married Ellen Martha, eldest daughter of Walter Rice Howell Barker of Wantage, and Robert Rowland Burton who died young in 1870, aged 18. John Robert Burton inherited Minera Hall estate from his father and died there in 1900, aged 50 years.

In 1808 an Act of Parliament was passed for the enclosure of 480 acres of common and waste land in the Parish of Minera. Some of this land was apportioned between Minera Hall and several other landowners in the Minera Parish.

During the early part of the 20th century a Mr Davison appears to have come into possession of the property, but documentary evidence is scarce. Between the two world wars Minera Hall was owned by a gentleman by the name of Mr Danson, who had been a tea merchant in India. He was a dapper little man with an oriental appearance. He was a benefactor to the village, donating financially to the various organisations in the village. He died at the Hall sometime in the 1950s and after his death a large auction sale was held on the premises to sell off all the furniture and household effects. The Hall and estate properties were sold at a later date. The property was purchased by the local branch of the Royal British Legion.

Minera Hall was built in a dressed buff-coloured sandstone from the local Berwig Quarry. The hall was approached by a carriage drive on a gradient through a wooded

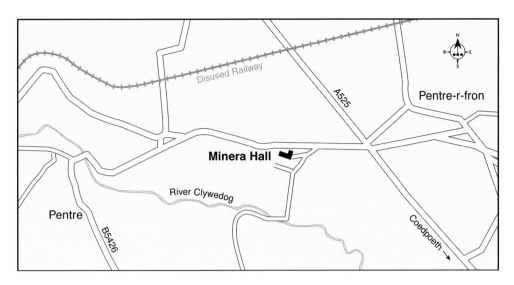

area of mature trees, leading through a pair of ornamental wrought-iron gates arriving in a natural court in front of the house, where an old sundial stood in the centre of a circular lawn. The house had a southerly aspect and was surrounded by about ten acres of land, stretching from the Minera Road down to the River Clywedog. The garden to the south elevation was landscaped in terraces and incorporated in the garden was a walled kitchen garden with two lean-to greenhouses. On the boundary to Minera Road was a high stone wall protecting the property.

According to the sale particulars of the property, the accommodation was as follows: library, drawing room with Lyncrusta ceiling and Adam frieze, inner hall with fine Minton tile floor, large dining room with two french windows giving access to the terrace garden, large study, butler's pantry, two kitchens leading to a walled-in yard giving access to dairy, boot room, coal house and wc. On the first floor, approached by a pitch-pine staircase, eight bedrooms, bathroom, housemaids' pantry, linen room and wc. On the second floor, five bedrooms, all approached by a secondary staircase.

In the adjacent stableyard was a stable for four horses, two loose boxes and coach-house. Connected to the Hall was a small farmery containing the following accommodation: trap-house, shippon for 16 cows, calf cote, mash-house, stable for two horses, two pigsties and large stockyard.

Publisher's Note: The author then wrote " Minera Hall is now vacant and I believe the property is due to be demolished in the near future." It is pleasing to report that it has been refurbished and is now in use as offices.

This attractive house was built in the 17th century in half-timber construction on a sandstone plinth. It stood on an elevated site overlooking the Alyn Valley, surrounded by mature trees and rhododendron shrubberies. The extensive views from the terrace garden over the Alyn Valley and Cheshire Plain were magnificent. Below the house was an expanse of meadow parkland stretching down to the home-farm; this was known as Yewtree Farm and was later a plant nursery farmed by Maitland Phillips.

There were two carriage drives leading to the house, one gave access from by the home-farm where a lodge was situated, the other gave access from Croes Howell hill near the coach-house and stable buildings. At this entrance was an unusual feature to one of the stone gate posts. The ornamentation to the recessed panel on the post has never been completed, owing to the death of the stonemason who was carrying out the work.

The first mention of any occupier to Mount Alyn was in 1776, when Anne, daughter of Walter Thomas of Chester, purchased the estate just before her marriage to Colonel Hugh Maxwell Goodwin; they both lived there for 66 years. Anne's uncle, Charles Goodwin, at that time lived at Burton Hall and had held the office of High Sheriff of Denbighshire in 1783. On his death Anne, his niece, inherited his estates, and when she married, her husband adopted the surname 'Goodwin' and became Maxwell Goodwin. He was a descendant of the family of Maxwell of Dalswinton, Dumfriesshire. During his army life he had served as Major on the staff of General Forbes for many years, connected with the 48th regiment.

In 1842, Anne died at the age of 85 years and left the Mount Alyn estate to her husband for his lifetime. He died in 1846. As there were no children, the Mount Alyn estate was inherited by the Rev. Roper Tyler. He took up residence there for a short time, but he sold the property to a Patrick Hunter and his wife Marie. She died there in September 1867 and was buried at Gresford.

After his wife's death, Colonel Maxwell Goodwin built a house in Gresford surrounded by 13 acres of land; the house was called 'Annefield' after his wife. His unmarried sister took up residence at 'Annefield', and, when he died in 1846, he bequeathed the property and land to his sister. Annefield was later owned by Col. Edward Dufre Townshend, who died there in 1883.

In 1869 Mount Alyn estate was purchased by Alexander Balfour, a Liverpool merchant and shipowner. He was a great benefactor to the City of Liverpool and Rossett. It was through his financial help that the Presbyterian Chapel, Institute and Cocoa Rooms were built in Station Road, Rossett; they proved a great asset to the village. It was through his enthusiasm that a number of boys from the village school were able to gain admission

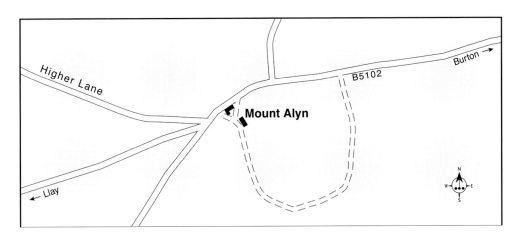

to the Conway Training Ship that was moored on the River Mersey in Liverpool. These boys gained their qualifications as Merchant Naval Officers and later played an important part in both World Wars.

Alexander Balfour resided at Mount Alyn for 17 years, travelling to Liverpool daily by train from Rossett Station. During the latter part of his life his health failed through cancer; an old friend of the family, Dr Thomas Keith, a surgeon from Edinburgh, carried out an operation on Mr Balfour at Mount Alyn. He survived the operation by three days, but died in April 1889, aged 62 years.

At the turn of the century Mount Alyn estate was purchased by J.W.Jolliffe of Liverpool, who completely rebuilt the house. During the 1930s the property was occupied by Captain Foulkes Roberts. The last owner-occupier of the Mount Alyn estate was William Cooper and his wife Elizabeth. He owned the sand and gravel quarries at Gresford and Rossett; during the construction of the Mersey Tunnel many tons of the material were dispatched by train from Rossett Station to Liverpool daily. The sand quarry which had been worked near Mount Alyn started to encroach on the land surrounding the property so the house was demolished in 1974.

Mount Street did not exist until the middle of the 18th century; the street was originally call "Love Lane" and at a later date the street was known as "The Green". In those early days The Green was one of the most desirable streets to live in. At the lower end of the street, the view was of green fields, stretching as far as the Caia Farm. At the other end of the street, towards The Nags Head public house, were some cottages belonging to the Pentrebychan Hall estate at Bersham. There were four large houses situated in Mount Street that had played a great part in the social life of the Wrexham. The first was The Mount, situated on an elevated site, which had derived its name from the street. The second was Mount Street House, which was situated on the same side as the Mount near The Nags Head. The third was Canarvon House, situated directly opposite The Mount on the other side of the street, and the fourth was known as The Office, situated where Salop Street meets Mount Street.

Mount Street House was built in a mellow reddish-coloured brick with some stone features, the low pitched roof covering the whole building in one span. The house was three storeys with sliding sash windows. To the front of the building were high wrought-iron railings set on a low curb, and the area between the railings and the house was planted with shrubs. At a later date the external elevations had been stucco rendered, when the house was remodelled.

Mount Street House was built about 1699 for Ellis Lloyd of Pen-y-lan estate, for his town house. Later the house was let to tenants. According to the Rate Book, the Lloyd family were still the owners of the property in 1715-1724. James Mytton was the first tenant; he had the lease on the property from 1724 and lived there until his death in 1737 but his widow lived on in the house until her death in 1749.

George Ravencroft took over the lease in 1750 and lived there until 1765 when he moved to Yspytty

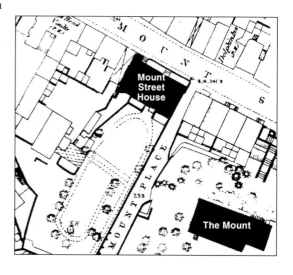

Uchaf, later known as Llwyn Isaf. George Ravencroft was a member of that family from Bretton near Chester.

Next to take up the tenancy was a curate from the Parish Church, the Rev. John Lloyd. He was followed as tenant by the Rev. John Yale, who was still tenant in 1793. The tenancy again changed hands in 1797 when George Kenyon, who was the second son of Roger Kenyon of Cefn Park estate, took it up. Roger Kenyon was an attorney at law, who had quite a large practice and had his office in the house at Cefn Park. In 1794 that house was destroyed by fire, many of the title deeds to the various properties in the area being burnt in the fire. Roger Kenyon was the brother of the first Lord Kenyon who married Mary Lloyd, the heiress to the Pen-y-lan estate.

In 1782 John Jones became owner of Mount Street House and on his death his son, William Jones, inherited the property. In 1808 the house came into the possession of another relative, Samuel Jones and in 1811 his son inherited it. John Jones was a surgeon and ran his practice from the house. He lived there until his death in 1824, aged 42 years. His widow lived on at Mount Street House for a period of twenty years after his death. Their son, William Denson Jones, was born there in 1802 and became a solicitor in Wrexham.

The property was then purchased by William Rowe, who was a civil engineer and surveyor. He had previously lived at The White House, Bersham. When Isaac Wilkinson first came to the Wrexham area from a village called Backbarrow, in the parish of Coulton-in-Furness, he brought with him a young man by the name of William Rowe to work for him as his surveyor and engineer. He stayed with the Wilkinson family until the business went into liquidation after the death of John Wilkinson.

William Rowe married Margaret Elizabeth, daughter of Thomas Jones, a gunsmith, who lived at the house called "The Greyhound" situated on Town Hill, Wrexham. William Rowe died in 1860, aged 71 years. There was one son to the marriage, John, who became manager of the Wrexham Gas Works, situated in Riverlet Road. This gas plant had been built on the site of the Dog Kennel Farm off Caia Road.

Mount Street House was assessed for the Hearth Tax as having twelve hearths. The property finished its days as the office building for Messrs F.W.Soames & Company, The Nags Head Brewery.

Another of the large houses situated in Mount Street was the property known as Carnarvon House; it belonged to the Broughton family of Marchwiel Hall estate and had been in the family for over a hundred years. It was the only property in Wrexham belonging to that estate. Over the years the house had been enlarged and renovated. The occupant of the house for many years was the second stepson of Sir Edward Broughton of Marchwiel Hall, Aquile Wyke, whose name is in the Rate Book as being in occupation in 1828.

The Mount was situated on an elevated site above Mount Street, from which it derived its name. At one time the property was known as Plas-y-Steward. It is mentioned that around 1524 the daughter of John ap Gruffydd ap David of Plas-y-Steward presented to St Giles Parish Church, Wrexham, a brass eagle lectern in memory of her family. The name of the house was later changed to The Mount.

The house was surrounded by a large garden with a spacious orchard, with access to Mount Street by a long flight of steps with landings at intervals. The stairway was divided into two near the street level; over this part of the stairway was a large oil-lamp supported by a strong iron frame.

The Mount was a tall narrow building of three and a half storeys, built in brick with stone features. The gable projected above the slate roof and was finished with coping stones and at the eaves, level to the roof, was a parapet wall. To the centre of the front elevation was a pediment gable and the central first floor window had a stone moulded surround with a pediment head.

The house had a history of eminent families who had lived there over the years. By the end of the 18th century The Mount had become a worthy and important edifice to the social life in the Township of Wrexham. Lady Eyton was one of the occupants in

1699; she was a member of the Eyton family from Leeswood Hall, Mold. She died at The Mount in 1767. Her husband Thomas Eyton had served at St Giles Parish Church in Wrexham as churchwarden in 1746-47. In 1787 the Rev. John Eyton MA, Rector of Erbistock, inherited The Mount. The property was then let to Robert Dodd on a tenancy of £40 per annum.

The property was inherited by Miss Anne Davies of the Mytton Davies family from Gwysaney Hall, Mold; she became locally known as "Madam Davies" and lived at The Mount with her companion, her sister Catherine. Catherine was Lady Williams, widow of Sir William Williams, Bart, of Plas Ward and was the fourth daughter of Mytton Davies. Miss Anne Davies died in 1749 and was buried in Mold churchyard.

The Mount was then inherited by the Rev. W.Eyton who sold the property in 1806 to Messrs John Samuel & Thomas Barker, merchants of Manchester, for the sum of £900. This was to defray Land Tax expenses that had accumulated on the Eyton Family estates.

By the early 19th century The Mount began to lose some of its former glory. The property started to show signs of neglect and in 1811 it was again sold to a group of business gentlemen who turned the house into a Working Men's Club and Institute, which was run very successfully for twenty-one years. The syndicate sold the property in 1892 for £1050 to the Ellesmere Railway Company. The money raised from the sale of The Mount was endowed in books for the Wrexham Free Library in the town.

Many historic houses were demolished in the locality of The Mount to make way for the railway which only survived for about 90 years.

The Nant-y-ffrith valley is a beautiful little valley situated at the base of Hope Mountain. It starts at the Ffrith Village and runs up to the lower reservoir on the Llandegla Moors. The little stream that runs through the valley is called Avon-y-ffrith and is the overflow from the reservoir. There are a number of spectacular waterfalls on the stream as it runs through the valley, and, where the stream passes the hall, it widens to form a shallow lake. Over the surface of the lake are water spouts fed by gravity from a pipe tapped into the stream higher up the valley.

The hall was situated half way down the valley surrounded by a plantation of trees mingled with rhododendron bushes. The approach to the hall was by a gravel carriage drive down the side of the valley; where the drive crossed the stream is a delightful stone bridge. The valley is said to be rich in lead ore and was worked by the Romans. Between the years 1735-57 some prospectors formed a company known as the Nant-y-ffrith Lead Mining Co., and they worked the valley for lead. A number of caves can be found on the side of the valley which are the remains of the lead workings. When one of the daughters from the estate married one of the Spottiswoods, the London Publishing House, one of the caves was fitted out with electricity and the reception held in the cave.

The hall was built in 1850 as a hunting lodge for a Liverpool gentleman by the name of Thomas Fry, who was related to the architects, A.P & H. Fry, who designed and built it. They also designed Bwlchgwyn Parish Church at about the same time. The property

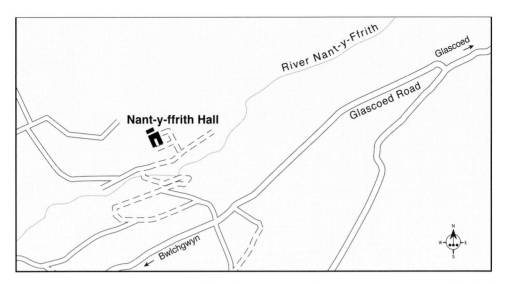

was built in dressed limestone and had been extended at various times. Part of the hall was two and a half storeys, the remainder two storeys and the greater part of the property was covered in a creeper. Within twelve months of the hall being completed, he sold it to another Liverpool merchant by the name of Mr Peek. In 1863 he sold the estate to R.V.Kyrke who bequeathed it to his son Richard Henry Venables Kyrke in 1883. Under his ownership the hall was extended and a great deal of landscaping carried out to the grounds surrounding the property. The house was so isolated that the owners of the hall had difficulty in keeping the domestic staff, but their rate of pay was much higher than the rest of the district. They employed a large staff inside and outside the hall. When the maids had their day off, the groom would take them in the pony and trap to meet the bus in the village and meet them in the evening when they were due back.

During the Second World War, Nant-y-ffrith estate was taken over by the military and used as an ammunition storage area. The hall and buildings were demolished between the years 1947-50. During my school summer holidays, my friends and I would walk for miles over the estate and we knew all the footpaths and got to know the estate staff. Before the war the hall and gardens would be open to the public one day in June. A garden party would be held on the lawn in front of the house with stalls round the perimeter. Games were organised for the children by the headmaster from the village school and jam and cream teas served in the Hall. That was a good day and everyone enjoyed themselves. Some silica mining was carried out in the valley at one time leaving unsightly rock faces; the estate was later taken over by the Forestry Commission who have now restricted access to part of the area. It all looks a sorry sight to those who knew the estate between the wars.

This attractive house was built on land on the outskirts of Ruabon village in the township of Morton Wallicorum, which had come into the possession of Sir Thomas Myddelton of Chirk Castle estate in 1667. The house was situated in the Parish of Ruabon and was called New Hall; it was built for his son Charles Myddelton at a cost of £1,144.13s.1d.

The hall was originally built in brick with stone features. Over the front entrance door cut into the stone was the coat-of-arms of the Myddelton family. Either side of the entrance were fluted columns and on the fine oak door were the initials "C.M" together with decorative wrought-iron work placed on the face of the door. Situated in the entrance hall was a fine Elizabethan carved oak staircase with pierced balusters; at first and second floor level were tall square newel posts to the staircase with pendants and finials. The ornamental plasterwork to the ceilings of the internal rooms was a fine example of the tradesmen's work in those days.

The house was a three storey building, the ornamental gables projected above the slate roof and at the eaves was a parapet gutter. The bold ornamental brick chimney stacks towered above the roof. The hall was assessed for the Hearth Tax as containing twelve hearths.

The hall was let on a lease to a family by the name of Captain Rice and his wife Mary

(nee Jones). He was for a number of years Adjutant with the Royal Denbigh Militia. He died there in September 1825, aged 67 years, but his widow, Mary, lived on in the hall until her death in October 1831, aged 73 years.

In 1839 New Hall was purchased by Henry Dennis from Colonel Cornwallis-West. Henry Dennis carried out a remodelling scheme to the hall, when the building was encased in stonework.

The Dennis family originated from an old Cornish family who worked the lead mines in that area. They came to the Wrexham area speculating in lead mining in the Minera and Nant-y-ffrith

area. The family branched out into the manufacture of bricks and tiles in the Ruabon area.

In more recent years the hall was purchased by the County Council and converted into a home for the aged before being demolished in 1950.

There is a stained glass memorial window in Ruabon Parish Church in the south aisle:

To the memory of Susan Hicks, wife of Henry Dennis, of New Hall, Ruabon, born 9th February 1839, died 26th April 1891.

Iwould suggest that the building dates back to the early 17th century, as there is no mention in the records that the house existed before 1663. It originally belonged to the Manley family of Manley Hall, Erbistock, and most likely could have been built for them. Sir Francis Manley used the property as his town house while on his business visits to Wrexham. He held the rank of Major in the King's army during the Civil War, but, unfortunately for the family, they fought on the losing side and had their estates compounded by Parliament and a fine of £75 imposed. He was knighted after the Restoration and the family carried on living at The Office for a number of years.

Over the years, The Office was let to a number of short-stay tenants. Kenrick Eyton of Eyton Isaf, Bangor-on-Dee, was charged for the rates on the property during the late part of the 17th century; afterwards his younger son Gerard Eyton was charged for the rates. He was a well-esteemed attorney in Wrexham who died at The Office in 1715 and was buried in Bangor churchyard. Dorothy Manley, widow of Sir Francis Manley, was the daughter of Sir Gerard Eyton. Gerard Eyton's widow, Anne, soon after the death of her husband, then married John Travers, one of the wealthiest men in Wrexham. This was his second marriage, let alone hers, and through the marriage The Office estate came into his possession.

From 1731 Dr. Lloyd, son of Foulk Lloyd of Foxhall, Denbighshire, occupied The Office until his death in 1734. The next tenant to occupy the property was Thomas Kyddyn of Maenan; he was connected with the family who owned Bryn Estyn. He was an attorney-at-law in the town, but he left The Office in 1744. The Rev. John Yale of Plas-yn-Yale, Bryn Eglwys, held the tenancy of The Office for a short time from 1768 to 1780. The next tenant was a lady by the name of Mrs Newton who occupied the house from

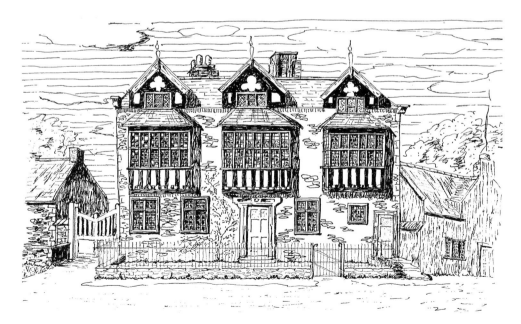

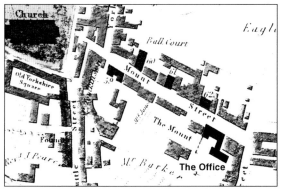

1781 to 1800 followed by Sam-uel Kenrick. A maltster by the name of John Parry was one of the last tenants. He served as a churchwarden at the parish church in 1801-02, and died in June 1810, aged 49 years. Shortly after this date The Office was demolished.

The Office was situated in the most desirable street in the town to live and played an important part in the social life of Wrexham. The house was a two and a half storey building built in a random rubble limestone to the lower part of the house. Part of the upper storey was of half-timber construction. The windows were a heavy timber frame with moulded mullions and transoms with leaded lights. The two massive stone chimney stacks were situated at the rear of the property. The front entrance was set central in the front elevation sur-rounded by a moulded stone frame. The house was set back from the roadway, with a small area of garden fenced off with wrought-iron railings set on a stone plinth. To the side of the building and to the rear stood the coach-house and stable accommodation. Access to the stable yard was by a pair of ornamental timber gates.

The old parsonage house to Rossett parish was built in 1866 at a cost of £1514. It was designed by the Chester architects Douglas & Fordham, who were also responsible for the design of Rossett Parish Church. The house was a two and a half storey building built in red brick with a slate roof. On the elevations was a pattern in blue brick, which was a typical feature in all John Douglas's designs. The vicarage was situated in about four acres of glebe land; a number of lovely mature trees adding to its garden setting. The garden had always been well maintained in the heyday of the vicarage, but in latter years the rhododendron bushes had grown wild. Part of the glebe was a field where the horses for the vicar's trap would graze.

The original approach to the vicarage was by a long carriage drive along the side of the churchyard giving access to the Wrexham to Chester Road. When the new church was built in 1892 the drive was resited with the access at Station Road opposite the Spar Shop. To the side and rear of the house stood a detached stable block with coach-house and stable for two horses and loose box, and over the stable were the living quarters for the coachman. In later years the stable block was converted into a meeting room for the church, and the accommodation over it was converted into the Youth Club meeting-room; the building was surrounded by a high brick wall which formed the stableyard.

The first incumbent of the new parish, when the church was first built, was an Irishman by the name of Rev. George Luthur Stone, who built his own vicarage some distance from the church along the Llay Road; he called the house "Stoneleigh".

The first vicar to occupy the new vicarage was the Rev. Thomas Vowler Wickham, who was the vicar responsible for the building of the new church. It was a sad beginning for

the church because the Rev. T.V.Wickham died just as the church was completed; when the Bishop of St Asaph came to consecrate the new church in the morning, he buried the vicar in the afternoon.

The next vicar to occupy the new vicarage was the Rev. Francis James (1892-1904), formerly of St Peters, Southampton. The vicar to succeed him was the Rev. Edward Charley (1904-23). The next vicar to follow was the Rev. Aneurin Davies (1923-36) who, during the 1914-18 war, had been a chaplain in the army and, while out in France, had become friendly with another army chaplain by the pet name of "Woodbine Willy", a name he acquired for his generosity in giving out cigarettes to the troops in the trenches. After the war Aneurin Davies invited "Woodbine Willy" to Rossett Parish Church to preach one Sunday evening. The church was filled to capacity for they had heard so much about the chaplain that the people of Rossett wanted to meet him.

The next vicar to occupy the vicarage was the Rev. Fred Phillips (1936-1948). He was succeeded as vicar by the Rev. Clifford Phillip Williams (1948-73), who left the parish to take up an incumbency at the Parish Church at Worthenbury where he died. The Rev. John Pugh succeeded him at Rossett (1973-83); he was formerly vicar of Bagilt Parish, Flint and later became a canon of St Asaph. On his retirement he moved to live in Wrexham where he died in 1996.

The Rev. Thomas Pierce, a much beloved vicar by the parish, was the last incumbent to occupy the vicarage; he lived there until 1989 when a new vicarage was built on the glebe, where he lived until his death in 1991.

The old vicarage was demolished about 1990 when the glebe land was sold by the Parsonage Board at Cardiff for development.

The site of the old vicarage belonged to St Giles Church, the parish church of Wrexham which dated back to the 13th century. The area on which the old vicarage stands and the area of Well Square are all part of the detached part of the Parish of Esclusion Below. It all formed part of the glebe land of about $1^{1}/_{2}$ acres.

The first vicarage to be built on the site was in 1661. This house would most likely have been built in half-timber construction; typical of so many houses to be found in this part of the township. The last vicar to reside in that house was the Rev. John Jones, who was succeeded by the Rev. Thomas Edwards who built a new vicarage on the same site. This house was built in brick with stone features and slate roof about the year 1732 and he was the only vicar to have lived continuously in the house until his death in 1770. He was buried in the chancel of St Giles Church, Wrexham, where a tablet to his memory can be seen.

The Rev. Thomas Edwards was succeeded as vicar of Wrexham Parish Church by the Rev. William Shipley, who took the title Dean Shipley. He was only in his 25th year when he became vicar of St Giles; his father was Doctor Jonathan Shipley, Bishop of St Asaph. In 1777 William married Penelope Yonge, the eldest of two daughters and co-heiress of Ellis Yonge of Bryn-Iorcyn and Acton Hall. Dean Shipley ultimately acquired Bryn-Iorcyn and other properties besides on the death of his father-in-law. He never took up residence at the old vicarage, but lived elsewhere on the outskirts of the town in one of his own properties. The senior curate lived in the old vicarage and ran the business of the church in the Dean's absence. It was general practice in those days for the vicar to live an independent life away from his church and install a curate to run its affairs in his absence, the vicar putting in an appearance about six visits a year.

Reginald Heber was born in 1783 and was educated at Whitchurch Grammar School, Salop. After his Oxford days he was offered the post of command of the Shropshire Volunteers, but his military career was brief and not a glorious one. He decided to take up holy orders. After he was ordained, he was appointed vicar of Hodnet parish in 1807-1823. During his military days he met at a dinner party Amelia Emily Shipley, daughter of Dr. Shipley, the Dean of St Asaph, and later they married. It was on one of his visits to the old vicarage at Wrexham that Reginald Heber wrote and composed the familiar hymn "From Greenland's icy mountains". In 1826 Dean Shipley died at the age of 56 years.

He was succeeded by Canon George Cunliffe, MA, who was the fifth son of Sir Foster Cunliffe, bart, of Acton Hall. He was born in 1795 and educated at Balliol College, Oxford. He was ordained priest in 1820 and two years later was appointed Rector of Petton in the diocese of Lichfield. He married Dorothea in 1821; she was the daughter of John Stanislaus Townshend of Trevalyn House, Allington. There was no issue from the marriage and she died in March 1877. Canon George Cunliffe abandoned the old vicarage and lived in his own property known as Llwyn Isaf, with access from Chester Street. When he died in 1875 he left Llwyn Isaf to St Giles Church to be used as the vicarage. George Cunliffe took up the incumbency at St Giles Church, Wrexham, in 1826.

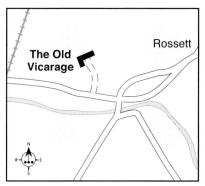

In the meantime the old vicarage had been let to various tenants and in 1880 the property was sold to the Wrexham, Mold and Connah's Quay Railway Company who used the premises as their offices. When the old vicarage was demolished the ornamental stone lintel from over the front door, which had been inscribed with the date, was removed to Llwyn Isaf and placed in the rock garden. The house was demolished in 1896 to make way for the construction of the Ellesmere Railway.

In an Ancient Terrier of 1870 the old vicarage was described as a mansion type house containing the following accommodation: sitting room built on to the end of the building as a lean-to, two parlours, one small and one large entertaining room (15ft by 10ft) – both rooms had a moulded cornice between wall and ceiling, a long passage or hall led through the house with access to the laundry (15ft by 10ft). There was a large brewing kitchen 15ft square with two cellars beneath. On the first floor were the usual lodging rooms with access from the landing, also a staircase to the garret rooms in the roof space. The panelled doors throughout the house were $2^1/_2$ inches thick with deep moulded architrave to the frames. At the rear of the property was a cobbled yard giving access to a stable for two horses and a loose box, also the coach-house together with other offices. Surrounding the house was a large garden incorporating an orchard and the whole was enclosed by a high stone and brick wall. The access to the vicarage was from Vicarage Hill. At one time the corner of Abbot Street and Vicarage Hill was known as Cuckoo's Corner but no-one seems to know why it was so called.

Overton Hall was a collection of rambling brick buildings, which had been added to over the years. The oldest part of the property was of half-timber construction and dated back to the 18th century. It was originally the old farmhouse and was situated to the rear of the site. The building was a two and a half storey house situated at the corner of Willow Street and the High Street, facing the Overton Parish Church. All the buildings had slate roofs with towering brick chimney stacks and, to one side of the building, was a huge lateral chimney stack. The property at one time belonged to the Gwernhaylod estate and the area of the holding was in the region of 84 acres.

The ground floor rooms had low open beam ceilings, the beams being stopped chamfered. Throughout the house were various exposed timber features, the partitions being wattle and daub. Some of the ground floor rooms were clad with splendid Tudor oak-panelling, other rooms had oak dado-panelling. The handsome oak carved staircase had moulded handrail with turned moulded balasters. The doors to the old part of the house were batten and braced, while the newer part of the hall had six panel doors, including the external door. The upper part of the hall had open timber roof trusses and purlins in fine condition.

During the period after the First World War (1914-18) a famous sporting personality by the name of Owen Wynn lived in the hall for a number of years. Prior to the Second World War (1939-45) a remarkable and talented sculptress, Miss Wyberge, occupied the hall. During her stay in the village she carried out a number of delightful carvings to the choir-stall in the parish church and also some worthy carved panelling in the village Cocoa-Rooms.

She was a very outgoing person and a good sportswoman, joining in the various events held in the village. In 1939 she volunteered and joined the A.T.S. and became the oldest serving woman member of the armed forces.

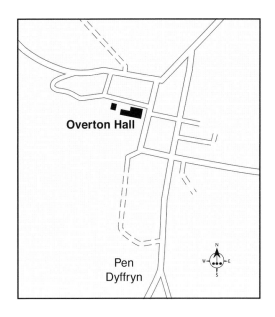

Overton Hall was demolished in 1965 to make way for a small housing development in the village.

The first recorded information of Parkey Hall was mentioned in 1657 when it formed part of the manor of Bedwell; the rates on the property at that time were paid by Captain Taylor, three shillings and three pence.

This late medieval house was built in two phases, one section was of cruck and box half-timber construction. The other section was constructed with close vertical studding, both methods having brick infill. At that time the roof would have been thatched. The lower section had dormer windows set into the roof and a brick chimney stack was set central of the ridge. Parkey Hall was a fine example of its period, but this type of construction today is very scarce. The hall is situated near to the River Clywedog in the Parish of Sesswick. The Parkey Hall estate was in the ownership of the Taylor family; Thomas Taylor was Mayor of Holt in 1650 and 1661.

During the Civil War, Captain Edward Taylor was the well-known Parliamentary Officer. He was the second son of Thomas Taylor of Dutton Diffaeth, yeoman. He married Katherian, daughter of Richard Presland the elder of Ridley Hall, a yeoman. The area of Parkey Hall estate was at that time 81 acres. In 1732 the estate was owned by John Taylor, the grandson of Captain Edward Taylor. In 1749, according to the Rate Book, the Taylor family were still the owners of the estate.

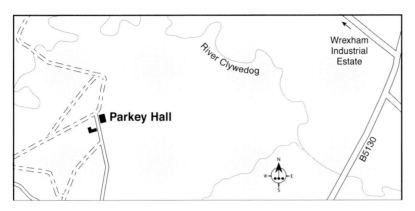

On the estate was situated Parkey Lodge which had 20 acres of land. This part of the estate was sold, the purchaser being John Puleston of Pickhill Hall. In 1789 Parkey Lodge was again sold to Owen Dodd of Sutton Green, and the Dodd family lived at Parkey Lodge for a short time after the purchase. Before very long the Dodd family were in financial straits and Parkey Lodge, with the 20 acres, was mortgaged twice over. In the meantime this property was let to a Lieutenant Johnson Butler Carruthers who held the tenancy from 1801 to 1805. In 1818 Edward Edwards was the new owner of Parkey Hall estate; he had bought the mortgage with the 20 acres and Parkey Lodge and added it to the main estate.

Edward Edwards' wife Margretta was the daughter of Owen Dodd. In 1827 the daughter of Edward Edwards junior, Caroline Thomas, sold Parkey Hall estate to Edward Lewis of St.Albans who sold it to Sir Robert A.Cunliffe of Acton Park. The hall at this time had been reduced in size, as some of the buildings had been demolished.

In 1939, at the beginning of World War Two, the estate was taken over by the Government on a compulsory purchase order for the building of the Ordnance Factory and the hall was left vacant during the war. The house soon became derelict and was demolished in 1972.

PENDINE HALL, STANSTY
(also Cae Bryn and Highfield)

The original house on the site dated back to the 17th century and was known as Cae Bryn. The estate came into the possession of the Owen family in 1780, when John Owen, a victualler from Ruabon, purchased the property. Before this time the farm was let on a tenancy to Ellis Jones, whose name is mentioned as having served as church-warden at Wrexham Parish Church in1769-70 while living at Cae Bryn.

Joshua Owen inherited the Cae Bryn estate from his father, then in 1814 the farm was sold with 14 acres of land to Richard Kyrke of Bryn Mali, Brymbo, and his wife Ellen Venables, who was the daughter of George Venables of Prestbury. Mrs Kyrke died in 1827, aged 82 years. Richard Kyrke carried out a remodelling scheme on the house and changed the name of the property to Highfield.

On the death of Richard Kyrke in 1839, Highfield was bequeathed to his daughter Margaret and her husband John Dickenson who was a well-known Wrexham surgeon. He was

renowned for being the first surgeon in the Welsh area to administer general anaesthetic in 1877. John Dickenson was elected Mayor of Wrexham in 1861 and died in 1877 at the age of 77 years. John Dickenson had his surgery in the Beast Market and, when he died, his grandson Dr Henry Venables Palin inherited the practice. He also was elected to the office of Mayor of Wrexham in 1889-90.

In 1881 the Highfield estate was put on the market by John Dickenson junior and sold to Major Evan Morris, a Wrexham solicitor who had been living at Roseneath, originally the residence of William Low, a local mining engineer. Evan Morris became Mayor of Wrexham in 1888 and, in the same year, was knighted by Queen Victoria at Pale Hall, near Bala, when she was on her visit to the Denbighshire area. When Sir Evan Morris died in 1890 the Highfield estate was let on a tenancy to W.F.Butler at an annual rent of £110. Sir Evan Morris was a member of the Morris family connected with the Cambrian Leather Works.

In October 1891 the High-field estate was again put on the market to be sold by auction at the Wynnstay Arms Hotel in Wrexham. The land was sold separately

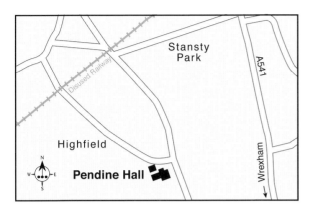

for building development, where 21 houses were built. This area formed a small hamlet to become known as Highfield, Stansty. The house was bought by Walter Pen Dennis, son of Henry Dennis of New Hall, Ruabon. Walter Pen Dennis was married to Jane Woodford (née Manton). There were three children to the marriage, two sons and one daughter. W.P.Dennis carried out extensive alterations and additions to the house; the interior was very grand with ornate plasterwork and panelling to the rooms. The name of the house was again changed to Pendine Hall.

The extensive garden surrounding the house was re-landscaped with rhododendrons, bushes and trees, and a large rock garden was laid out with a wishing well. An unusual summer-house was built in the garden; circular in plan, it was built in random rubble stone of two storeys. Access to the first floor was by a cantilever stone stairway and the circular terrace to the first floor was supported on stone corbels guarded by a wrought-iron handrail. The pyramid slate roof had a steep pitch, with a brick chimney projecting from the side of the roof. The whole structure had a rugged appearance.

In 1921 Pendine Hall was again put on the market to be sold by auction at the Wynnstay Arms Hotel in Wrexham. The property did not reach the reserved sale price and was withdrawn from the sale. The Dennis family continued to live at the hall until 1929; just before that Walter Pen Dennis died at the hall in February 1928. Between the years 1930-34 Duncan Robertson and his wife Joyce, who was a daughter of Sir Watkin William Wynn, lived at the hall.

Duncan was the son of Henry Robertson of Llantysilio Hall. In 1936 Nichacle Christian Dennis was in occupation at Pendine and later on in 1939 Elizabeth Grant and Eileen Morris were the occupants of Pendine Hall.

In 1940 the hall was taken over, for the duration of the war, by St Monica's R.C.School who were evacuated from Croydon.

In 1949 the hall was purchased by Mr & Mrs J.W.Finch who had two children. They converted the house into a residential hotel and riding school. On a Sunday evening in April 1958 the property was burnt to the ground. Only the tower and part of the new extension built by Mr Dennis remained; there was nobody in the hall at the time.

Pentrebychan estate in the early 16th century belonged to the Tegin family of Bron-deg. In 1507 Richard Tegin accepted the office of Sergeant-at-Arms with the Tudor monarchy and was living in the old house at Pentrebychan. In 1620 he sold Pentrebychan estate to Hugh Meredith who was the first Meredith to own and live there.

The original house on the site was a long single storey dwelling, 'L' shaped in plan. It was built in half-timber construction with wattle and daub infill and the roof was thatched. The old house was demolished in 1823 when a new house was built on the same site. It was a large square block with small gables to all elevations and was built in dressed stone with stone mullion windows. It is believed to be the work of William H.Gummow, the Wrexham architect and builder. During the construction of the hall part of Offa's Dyke had to be levelled out to form the garden. At the rear of the house was built a stable block and coach-house. The house was surrounded with a spacious garden with mature trees; in the garden stands a circular brick-built dovecote dating back to 1721, believed to be still standing.

Ellis Meredith, son of Hugh Meredith 2nd, inherited the estate from his father and he married Elizabeth, daughter of Hugh Currer of Greys Inn, London. Ellis Meredith served as churchwarden at St Giles Church, Wrexham in 1686-87 and died in 1718. He was a merchant tailor in London. Although he owned Pentrebychan, he never lived there, as he also had a town house in Chester Street in Wrexham, the site of which became Lloyds Bank.

Dr Thomas Meredith inherited the estate; he was the second son of the 2nd Thomas Meredith of Pentrebychan Hall and died in 1802, aged 42 years. He was the last in the male line of the Merediths of Pentrebychan Hall.

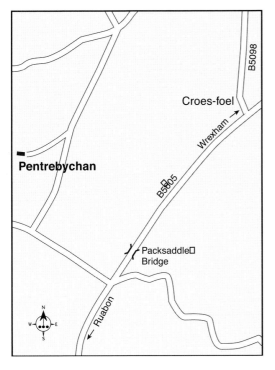

The estate was then inherited by Henry Warter, son of Joseph Warter of Sibberscot in Shropshire. He had married Margaretta, daughter of the 2nd Thomas Meredith and heiress of her brothers Richard and Thomas Meredith, assumed by Royal Warrant on this inheritance of the Pentre-bychan Estate. He adopted the name Meredith in addition to his own and married Elizabeth Lowry, daughter of Mongo Park, the explorer, and was father of the Lieut. Col. Meredith also of Pentrebychan Hall, who died in 1879. He had served as churchwarden at St Giles Church in 1829-30.

The Pentrebychan estate had many properties in Wrexham; it was a scattered estate and was eventually sold off. In 1962 the hall was purchased and demolished by the Council and the site became the Wrexham Crematorium. The last occupant of the Hall was Professor Share-Jones who was the Professor of the Veterinary Department at Liverpool University.

Plas Acton was built about 1860 for John James who was one of the leading lawyers in the town. He was the son of Thomas James of Wem, Salop, who started the law partnership of James & Hatch in 1823 and whose offices were situated in the old Gate-House in Priory Street, Wrexham.

John James was married three times, first to Mary Anne, daughter of John Painter, the printer, who had his shop in High Street, Wrexham. Their marriage lasted eight years until her death in 1824. In 1838 John married his second wife Catherine, a daughter of Thomas Hilditch of Oswestry. This marriage lasted only a short time until she too, died. He was married a third time, to Anne Elizabeth, daughter of John Farrer who was at that time manager of the Kenrick & Bowman Bank, which was also located in High Street, Wrexham.

John James and family were staunch Presbyterians and he was at one time one of the trustees for the Chester Street Presbyterian Chapel. At one time he was chapel organist for a number of years and during this time (in 1836) he presented to the chapel a much larger pipe organ which he purchased from St Mark's Church in Liverpool.

In his younger life John James set up a law partnership with an up-and-coming lawyer, Cyril Jones. The partnership did not last long, because shortly afterwards John joined his father's practice at the Gate-House, hence the name of the partnership – James, James & Hatch.

Plas Acton House was built in a mature reddish brick with stone features; it was a house of character with many interesting and historical features. The house was situated within a large mature garden, the land attached to the dwelling being in the region of about 25 acres. The approach to the house was by a curved carriage drive leading from Pandy Lane. At the rear of the property was a cobbled courtyard giving access to the stable and coach-house. The slate roof to Plas Acton had an interesting profile, with a steep pitch of about 60 degrees. There were many gables to the roof with ornamental bargeboards. The tall ornamental brick chimney stacks towered above the roof and were capped with moulded stone coping.

The projecting stone-built bay window to the front elevation was a novel feature with stone mullions and transoms, and a castellated finish to the top of the bay. The project-

ing porch was also built in stone, its
steep gable projecting above the roof
level and finished with moulded coping stones. The pointed moulded arch
gave character to the place of entry. The
name of the architect is not known, but
resembles the work of Mr Gummow.

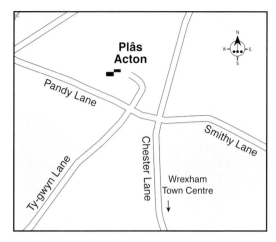

When the Wrexham Corporation
received its Charter in 1857, it was a
turning point in the history of the town.
The division of the electoral wards had
not yet come about until the year 1876,
when the election of the first Council
took place. There were fifty-two names put forward as candidates, out of which twelve
were elected to serve on the new Council. John James was elected the first Town Clerk to
the Corporation at a salary of £80 per annum. He continued in that office until he resigned
in the March of 1879. At that time the Council meetings were held in Bryn-y-ffynnon
House which was taken over for the Municipal Offices. John James was succeeded by
Thomas Bury. John James after an interesting life died at Plas Acton in the May of 1888
and was buried in Gwersyllt Churchyard. His father-in-law John Farrer also died at Plas
Acton in December 1882, aged 85 years.

In 1929 Plas Acton was purchased by the law partnership of Cyril Jones and the property
was then let to various short stay tenants. During the war years (1939-45), the house was
let to evacuees by the name of Wiles. By the end of the war the property needed money
spending on maintenance work, to bring it up to some sort of standard.

In 1945 the property was put on the market to be sold by auction at the Wynnstay Arms
Hotel, Wrexham by the auctioneers Seth Hughes & Co. The property was purchased
by the Eames family for the sum of £1,000. Mr Austin Eames, the well known electrical
engineer in the Wrexham area, took up residence at Plas Acton. Mr Peter Eames, who
kindly lent me the photograph of the house, informed me that the house was divided into
two during the early part of the 20th century, the rear part of the house being known
as Acton House. He also mentioned that the name of Eames was a Cornish name, his
ancestors originating from Cornwall.

The Eames family lived at Plas Acton until it was purchased by the Welsh Board in
1970 on a compulsory purchase order for the route of the proposed Gresford, Flossett
and Pulford bypass. The house and buildings were demolished just after this date when
work started on the bypass. Thus another lovely old house was removed from the landscape in the Wrexham area in the name of progress.

During the latter part of the 16th century the large estate of Plas Cadwgan formed part of the manor of Esclusham; this land was in the possession of one of the Welsh tribes that had descended into the area from Cynwrig of Rhiwallon. The Plas Cadwgan estate was inherited by a family known as John ap Davis ap Robert, and the sons of the family adopted the name of Jones. It was the eldest son of the family, Edward Jones, who inherited the estate after his father's death. He was an important man in the area and at one time held the post of Master of the Wardrobe to Queen Elizabeth I. He also held the office of High Sheriff of the County of Denbighshire. The younger son, who was also called Edward, inherited Plas Cadwgan on his father's death. The son liked a social life and mixed in high society; he had a number of young friends, two of whom where Thomas Salusbury of Llewnni and Anthony Babington of Wirksworth, Derbyshire. Between them they formed a secret society led by Anthony. Their intention was to actuate a plot to remove the Queen from the throne of England and place on the throne in her stead, Mary, Queen of Scots. In 1586 the plot was discovered and all the members of the society were arrested and put in the Tower of London. Anthony Babington was arrested in London, his two colleagues, Salusbury and Jones escaped to Cheshire, but were arrested later. They were tried for treason and executed. The family lost their estates to the Crown.

Not long after the death of Edward Jones, Plas Cadwgan estate came into the possession of the Cure family. George Cure took over the estate from his father Thomas Cure in about 1588. He married Ellen, one of the daughters of Owen Brereton of Borras Hall and there was a son and daughter to the marriage. The daughter Anne married Captain Roger Myddelton and came into possession of Plas Cadwgan estate in 1620, where they took up residence.

The estate remained in the Myddelton family until the late 18th century, when Richard Myddelton died in 1796 without issue. The Plas Cadwgan estate was then put on the

market and sold to Thomas Fitzhugh of the Plas Power estate.

When the Hearth Tax was enacted, Plas Cadwgan was assessed as containing 16 hearths. This shows the extent of the house which covered a large amount of ground. Part of the dwelling was built in half-timber construction and part in random rubble limestone. This 14th century dwelling was a fine example of the aisle-truss

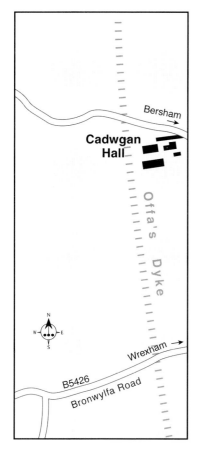

construction; it was one of the best preserved half-timber and stone built houses of its period. There had been various additions to the hall over the centuries and there were two wings with a central portion. The central part and the north wing were demolished in the early 19th century, leaving the south wing. The stone arched porch and entrance hall formed part of this wing. The entrance hall contained a fine oak staircase; this room was used as the kitchen. The room had an open ceiling to the carved roof trusses, the space between the timbers being in ornamental plasterwork.

During my research on the estate an interesting note came to light in one of the historical journals. During an early archaeological dig on a large tumulus situated within the curtilage of the hall, about 1797, the skeleton of a large horse was found; the bones were in good preservation and on its feet were iron horse shoes of rough workmanship. They also found four suits of armour complete with helmets and gorgets. At the time the suits of armour were taken to Chirk Castle for safe keeping. When at a later date enquiries were made about the whereabouts of the suits of armour, nothing could be found.

Down through the ages Plas Cadwgan had been let to various tenants; John Owen had lived in part of the hall and died there in 1718 – he had served as churchwarden at St Giles Parish Church in 1702-03. In the late 18th century John Rogers was tenant; he had also served as churchwarden at St Giles in 1770-71. Another tenant was Richard Edwards who died there in 1823, aged 61 years; he was also churchwarden at St Giles in 1823.

Within the curtilage of the hall in the yard at the rear of the property was a stone-built building. The building had been used as a barracks to house the estate soldier-retainers in bygone days. During the early 20th century the owner of the estate wanted to demolish the house. He met a great deal of opposition from various quarters. Eventually he won his request and the hall was demolished in 1967, including the barracks. Many photographs were taken of the hall and drawings made for future records. The timber trusses and part of the half-timber structure were reassembled at the Avoncroft Museum in Bromsgrove.

Plas Coch was built in the late 16th century in a mature hand-made red brick, which gave the house its name (redhouse). It was a two storey house and the plan of the dwelling was a typical through passage house with access at either end of the passage. This passage divided the main living room or hall from the service rooms, rather than the byre as in the long Welsh house (see plan across). Plas Coch had been extended in the 19th century and renovated internally. At the rear of the dwelling was a lateral chimney stack and a smaller lateral chimney stack was set against the gable end. The house had been assessed for the Hearth Tax as containing nine hearths. At one period the elevations had been stucco rendered with mock half-timber working to the upper storey.

The house was originally built for William Meredith in 1592, who was knighted later in life. He was one of the sons of Richard Meredith of Allington Hall. Edward Meredith, a brother to William, was recorded in 1610 as trading as a draper in Cheapside, London, and he had held the lease on Plas Coch from his nephew for a time. Sir Richard Meredith held the office of High Sheriff of Denbighshire in 1629. The land within the curtilage of the house and buildings was in the region of 76 acres, with an additional 43 acres of land situated in Broughton.

One of the daughters of Hugh Meredith of Pentrebychan Hall, Mrs Ermine Hadilo took over the lease on Plas Coch in 1660; she was the widow of Arthur Hadilo, MA. who

had been Rector of Denbigh Parish Church in 1633-36. After the death of Mrs Hasilo, her daughter Jane Hadilo occupied Plas Coch until 1694. Next to take over the tenancy was a Samuel Powell paying a rent of £47.6s.8d. per annum. In 1698 Katherane Eyton became tenant of Plas Coch and lived there for a short time only until her death. The tenant to follow her in 1699 was Anthony Townshend, who was the son of Sir Robert Townshend of Trevalyn House, Allington.

In 1709 the Plas Coch estate was sold by William Meredith of Kent, the purchaser being Sir John Wynn of Gwydir Hall, Llanrwst. The property was then let to a number of farming tenants, descendants of the Samuel family, for over a hundred years. The first was Watkin Samuel whose name is mentioned in the record of St Giles Parish Church as having served as churchwarden in 1756-57; he died at Plas Coch in 1786. His son succeeded him as the next tenant and was also called Watkin Samuel; he farmed the holding until his death in 1811, aged 52 years. His son took over the tenancy from his father and was also churchwarden at the parish church in 1826-27.

Plas Coch played an important part in the social life of the town. After the Second

World War the Denbighshire & Flintshire Agricultural Society held their show on part of the land. The house and buildings were demolished to make way for a large development of supermarkets and a technical college. The only part of the property remaining is a short length of stone wall at the roadside in front of 'Homebase'.

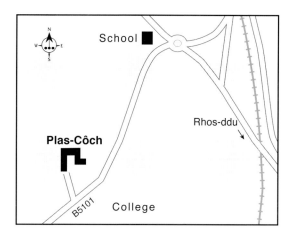

Inside the house were some remarkable exposed timber features, moulded oak beam open ceilings and the massive moulded oak front door frame with its heavy studded oak door – we shall not see such workmanship again.

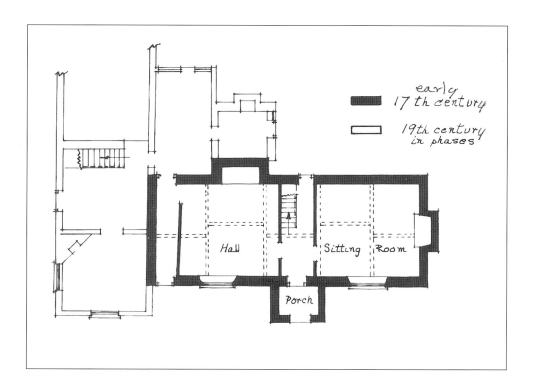

Plas Fron was originally built in 1657 to a classical design for a gentleman by the name of Mr Holbrook. Little is known about him or the house during this period. Plas Fron was sold by Mr Holbrook in 1694 and purchased by Weston Hassall. The family lived there until Mr Hassall died. He was buried in Bangor churchyard.

The estate was later inherited in 1811 by Edward Edwards who owned Parkey Hall, Sesswick. He was a relative of the Hassall family. The Edwards family lived at Plas Fron for a number of years.

In 1891 Plas Fron estate was purchased by Sir Roger Palmer of Cefn Park, from Mr J.R.Bennion. It is said that the property was given to a relative of the Palmer family as a wedding gift. In 1895 Captain George C.Fenwick had some connection with Plas Fron estate.

In the Parish Church of Bangor a brass plaque may be seen bearing the following inscription:-

"In memory of Private Roger Mansell William Fenwick, the younger son of Mrs Mary Fenwick of Plas Fron, and the late Captain G.C.Fenwick, R.W.F. 1914-18."

Plas Fron was built in brick with stone features to a classical design. An extension to the rear of the property was carried out in 1912; this was a two storey building while the rest of the house was a three storey building. The roof to the original part of the house was a shallow pitch and to the front elevation was a shallow projection capped by a pediment gable. This was the only gable to the house and the roof had a hip construction. The bold brick chimney stacks towered above the roof. The gardens surrounding the house were landscaped in a very formal manner with low box hedges and shrubs. The garden, about an acre, was always well-maintained.

To the south of the house was a cobbled yard giving access to the coach-house and stable block. A small stream called "The Foss" passed within a few yards of the property. There was quite a long carriage drive from the Bangor Road to Plas Fron.

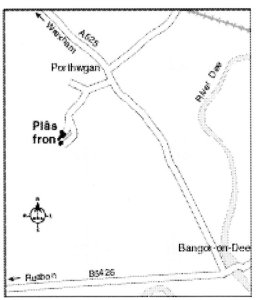

Plas Grono is an abbreviation of the name Plas Goronwy and the property was originally called Ty-Cerryd. The estate was purchased by Elihu Yale, great grandfather of Dr David Yale, who was one of the younger sons of the Plas-yn-Ial family at Bryn Eglwys in the 16th century. As the Yale family lived abroad a great deal of the time, Plas Grono estate was rented out to various tenants.

David Yale is mentioned in the Register of Wrexham Parish Church as having served as Churchwarden in 1673-74. He died at Plas Grono in 1690 and was buried in Wrexham Churchyard. David Yale was a very young child when he emigrated to America with his stepfather Theophilus Eaton, a strict Puritan. They made the crossing seventeen years after the Mayflower landed with the first settlers in America. In 1641, at the age of 27, David moved to Boston, Massachusetts, where he became a prosperous merchant and married

his wife, Ursula. It was here that Elihu was born in April 1649; he was the second son. In 1651 the family left Boston for the old country and took up residence at Plas Grono, which David had inherited from his father. Elihu was now three years old. Their stay at Plas Grono was not long, and the family moved to London where Elihu received his education. David Yale died at Plas Grono in 1690 and was buried in Wrexham Churchyard.

In the December of 1671, Elihu was offered a post with the East India Company as a writer and remained with the company for twenty-seven years. On receiving promotion in 1672 he moved to Madras. By the year 1684 he was appointed Acting Governor and three years later Governor of Fort St.George. In the February of 1699 he decided to return to the old country on a ship carrying a rich and valuable cargo. A wealthy man, in our day and age he would be considered a multi-millionaire. In the November of 1680 Elihu married a widow, Catherine Hynmer, who had four children. When they returned to the old country he and Catherine lived separate lives. Elihu died in 1721 and Catherine died in 1728 aged 77 years. In the year 1704 Elihu Yale was appointed High Sheriff of the County of Denbighshire.

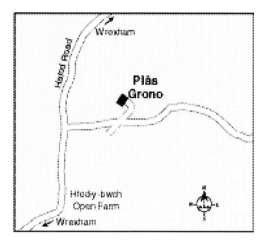

Plas Grono was a double structure of two and a half storeys, the front elevation was in three bays capped with three gables, and at the end was attached a large lateral chimney stack which towered above the slate roof.

Watt's Dyke is very close to the house and the property adjoins the Erddig estate parkland which was at that time owned by Joshua Edisbury. When he became financially embarrassed during his ownership of Erddig, Elihu Yale lent him money for the estate not long after his return from the Far East. A short time later the mortgagees foreclosed on the estate thus forcing Joshua Edisbury into bankruptcy.

Round about 1760, Isaac Wilkinson held the tenancy of Plas Grono for a short time, after he came to the area from the parish of Cartmel then in North Lancashire. In 1774 the lease on Plas Grono was taken over by the Rev. George Warrington, who later became vicar of Hope. Following him as tenant was Thomas Apperly and, in 1777, his son Charles was born there. Charles Apperly became the famous sports writer under the name of "Nimrod". The next tenant was Thomas Jones of Llanerchaugog Hall, who was the owner of Llwyn Enion Iron Works. He had served as churchwarden at Wrexham Parish Church in 1818-19. The next tenant recorded was Alexander Ellis who also served as churchwarden in 1815-16. Then came William Bennion, who was a leading lawyer in the town; he served as churchwarden in 1827-28. The last tenant was John Dickin, a tanner, who lived at Plas Grono for a number of years. In 1876 the house was demolished and two cottages were built on the site. Plas Grono now forms part of the Erddig estate.

Plas Gwern was originally built as a town house for Sir Richard Trevor of Trevalyn Hall, Allington. The house was first known as Y-Bryn which was later changed to Plas Gwern. The layout of the plan was "E" shaped. It was built in half-timber construction in box framing with brick infill. Attached to the rear of the house was a brick-built kiln. The dwelling was built on an elevated site close to the rear of the oldest public house in the town, The Nags Head. Plas Gwern was a two storey building with the stable and barn incorporated at the end of the building. A small garden was attached to the property and close by Plas Gwern were three cottages belonging to the same estate. They faced Tuttle Street and overlooked the little timber bridge spanning the River Gwerfro, the bridge being known as "Y-bont bren". It was later replaced with a stone built bridge and the name changed to "Pont Tuttle". Plas Gwern was steeped in history and played an important part in the social life of Wrexham.

The first recorded occupant of Plas Gwern was Mrs Elizabeth Jones who was a very generous person in the parish. On her death in May 1668, she bequeathed the sum of thirty-four shillings to be donated yearly to the poor of the parish, this legacy being the rent from a smallholding situated in the Beast Market area in Wrexham Abbot. This holding was in the tenure of Michael Davies in about the year 1770-71. Also mentioned in her will, as one of her heirs, was Thomas Pulford, who belonged to one of the leading families in the township of Wrexham.

Plas Gwern had a number of short stay tenants. The property was let to George Blac-kborne from 1703 to 1706. He married Margarete, daughter of Thomas Powell of Hosely Hall, Marford. When the family moved from Plas Gwern, they took up residence at a house in Marford known as Roft-y-Castell where he held the office of Steward for the manor of Hosely and Marford in the parish of Gresford. He later became the agent to the Trevalyn Hall estate, when he moved to live in Trevalyn Hall in 1725. In 1714 his son Thomas Blackborne married Elizabeth, daughter of Thomas Rosindale of Chester Street, Wrexham. The couple went to reside at Plas Gwern. Thomas lost his wife in 1755 and he died not long afterwards in 1760. They had no children.

Near the end of the 18th century Plas Gwern was purchased by the Davies family who owned The Nags Head pub in Mount Street. In 1747 the tenancy changed to William Jones who was a wine and spirits merchant. His shop was on the corner of Abbot Street and Blackchamber Passage and was called The Vaults. During the period between 1752 and 1764 a Miss Powell held the tenancy of Plas Gwern; she was a maiden lady and lived

The house surrounded by beer barrels. It is in a derelict condition and the photograph must have been taken shortly before demolition

there for twelve years before she died. She was the last in the line of the Powell family of Broughton Hall, Southsea.

The tenant to follow Miss Powell was John Kenrick junior, of Wynne Hall, Ruabon, who kept it as his town house. In 1773 the owner of Plas Gwern, Miss Davies of The Nags Head, put the property up for auction at The Nags Head. The sale particulars on the property described the house as: "a desirable town house with stable, coach-house, barn and kiln, freehold." On the same day as the sale, two fields known as "Cae Denter" and "Pen Crach" were put up for auction together with eight small terrace houses.

Plas Gwern failed to reach the reserve sale price and was withdrawn from the sale. Mr Kenrick remained the tenant and Miss Davies the owner.

The next tenant of Plas Gwern was Edmund Jones who was a grazier of cattle. According to the Register at Wrexham Parish Church he had served as churchwarden in 1785-86. By this time Plas Gwern had lost most of its former glory and had become neglected by the owner and the tenant. The property fell into disrepair and eventually Plas Gwern was demolished in 1888 to make way for The Nags Head Brewery, owned by Frederick William Soames, of Bryn Estyn, Bieston (see page 20). It was a sad end to such a remarkable house.

The original house built on the site of Plas Madoc was a half-timber constructed dwelling, built in 1455 for Madoc ap David ap Llewelyn ap Ednyfed. John Lloyd, who was descended from that family, was the first to adopt the surname of Lloyd, and was responsible for building the new house on the site of the old one. He married Janet, daughter of Geoffrey Bromfield of Bryn-y-Wiwer, Ruabon. He lived at Plas Madoc in 1546 and died there in 1564.

In 1620 Edward Lloyd inherited Plas Madoc estate; he was a coroner and a grandson of John Lloyd. The estate at that time had increased in size to $232^{1}/_{2}$ acres and the house had been assessed for the Hearth Tax as containing seven hearths. Edward died in 1636 and was buried at Ruabon. His eldest son died in his father's lifetime but his other son, also named Edward, inherited the estate.

It was in 1773 that Sarah Edwards of Crogen, Glynceiriog, inherited Plas Madoc. She was also heiress of Clochfaen and was the widow of John Edwards of Crogen. In 1773 she married the Rev. Thomas Youde and there were six children to the marriage. Harriet was the youngest of the family and sole heiress. She married a Captain Jacob William Hinde, who was an obsessive gambler and within a short time gambled away Plas Masoc in 1858. The estate had been mortgaged for a number of years to George Hammond Whalley and in 1858, George Whalley foreclosed on the mortgage. After a great deal

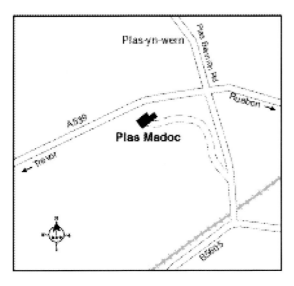

of discussion between the trustees of T.W.Youde and G.H.Whalley, it was agreed that G.H.Whalley would purchase Plas Madoc estate offering the best price to pay off the debts. Sarah lived on at Plas Madoc until her death in December 1837, when G.H.Whalley took up residence. He died there in October 1878, and it was he who extended the house by building the odd structure at the end of the property.

George Hammond Whalley held the office of High Sheriff of the County in 1856 and became Liberal M.P. for Peterborough in 1852-74. He was dubbed the laird of Plas Maggot.

It was through the efforts of G.H.Whalley in Parliament that the toll-gates were removed from the country roads. A haulage contractor, working from the Kings Mills area in Wrexham, earned his living from carts and horses travelling the roads and had a saving of £200 a year when the toll-gates disappeared.

Plas Madoc estate was inherited by General De Wat, one of the leaders of the Boer War era. He became commander-in-chief of the expeditionary force during the South African War. He was born in South Africa and his real name was George Hammond Whalley, heir to the Plas Madoc estate.

A number of tenants rented the hall during his ownership, one of the last occupiers being Charles Morris who was secretary of the old firm of Hughes & Lancaster in Acrefair. Another tenant to follow was John Jones, Headmaster of Rhos-y-Medre Church School.

After the death of G.H.Whalley, the Plas Madoc estate was sold to Sir Watkin Williams Wynn of the Wynnstay estate. The house had been vacant for a number of years and became derelict and was demolished in 1960. The site has now been developed as a council housing estate with a leisure centre.

The house was built in dressed stone with a parapet gutter to the slate roof. The house was of a pleasing design, except for the addition at one end of the house which completely spoilt the proportions of the building.

This early Renaissance dwelling subsequently came into the possession of William Santhey, who in 1655 sold the estate to Archdeacon William-Mostyn, from whom the house derived its name. The house was built on an elevated site exposed to the elements. The house had sweeping views and could be seen for miles around. The dwelling was known locally as Plas Mostyn Mawr, to distinguish it from another holding in the area known as Plas Mostyn Bach.

The house was built of limestone in random rubble with walls of great thickness. The dwelling was a double square pile with central lead valley. It had a slate roof with brick chimney stacks at each gable. A poor job had been made of the foundations on the sloping ground, for the whole of the structure showed signs of settlement and bulging walls not long after it was built. The building had been substantially buttressed even as early as 1791, the house being shown on a sketch of that date by the artist John Ingleby.

The stout castellated porch was built at a later date to the height of the second floor windows; this served as a buttress to the front elevation. The windows through the house were small with segmented half-brick arches and brick sills. The house was three and a half storeys in height and according to the assessment for the Hearth Tax the house contained six hearths. In the year 1670 the rent for the estate was four shillings and eight pence. By the year 1715 the rent had increased to £1. 3s. 8d.

In the year 1708 Roger Mostyn inherited Plas Mostyn from his father the Archdeacon, but shortly after, the Mostyn family ceased to live at Plas Mostyn. Roger Mostyn was

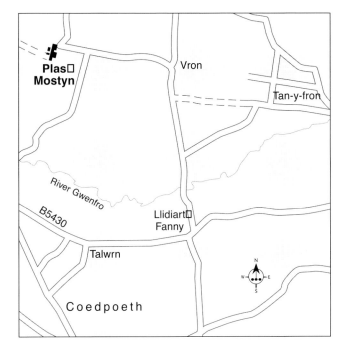

High Sheriff of Den-bighshire in 1689. The Mostyn family still retained the ownership of the estate but leased the house and land to Edward Parry who was the first tenant farmer on the estate. He is mentioned in the Register at the Parish Church at Wrexham as having served as Churchwarden in 1728-29 and died at Plas Mostyn in 1766.

In the year 1789 the estate came into the possession of Roger Kenyon of Cefn Park, Abenbury. On his death, Plas Mostyn was bequeathed to his younger son Thomas Kenyon. On his death, the estate was in-herited by Edward Kenyon, the area being about 156 acres. In 1812 the tenancy of was taken over by Richard Morris, who also served as Churchwarden in 1822-23. Richard Morris died at the house in 1847.

The Plas Mostyn estate was put on the market in 1847 and sold by auction at the Cross Foxes Inn, Coedpoeth. It was purchased by John Burton of Minera Hall. The property was leased to John Wynne who farmed it for a number of years. John Burton died in 1860. At a later date the tenant, John Wynne, bought Plas Mostyn and a new house was built on a more sheltered site in Ruabon red-pressed brick some time prior to the First World War. On John Wynne's death, his son Walter Wynne inherited the estate. Just after the end of the Second World War, the estate was worked for open-cast coal mining and reinstated on completion. The old stone house was demolished during this period, c.1950.

The first house to be built at Bersham was an attractive half-timber constructed dwelling with wattle and daub infill. It was built in the middle of the 15th century and was known as Ty-Bellot, after the name of the family who lived there. Robert Bellot occupied the house; he was the second son of Roger Bellot and was the great nephew of Bishop Bellot, Bishop of Chester and previously Vicar of Gresford. He died at Ty-Bellot in 1596 and was buried in the chancel of St Giles Church, Wrexham.

Robert Bellot married Jane, widow of Thomas Goldsmith and daughter of Edward Puleston of Llwyn-Cnottiau. In 1637-38 Robert served as churchwarden at St Giles Church, Wrexham. The Bellot family had an income from a number of corn mills which they owned in the Wrexham area together with the income received from the tolls of the various markets and fairs held in the Wrexham Township around 1623.

The Power family inherited the estate and changed the name of the house to Plas Power. Sir Henry Power of Bersham was created Viscount Valentia in Ireland in March 1620. He married Gressel, daughter of Sir Richard Bulkeley of Beaumaris, Anglesey. Sir Henry died at Plas Power in 1641 without issue.

Mary Myddelton of Croes Newydd came into possession of the Plas Power estate and, on her death in 1747, bequeathed the estate at Bersham to William Lloyd, son of the Rev. Thomas Lloyd. In 1757 the original house at Bersham was demolished and a new one built on the same site for William Lloyd. The house was built in a plain brick with stone features, a stone balustrade at eaves level and bold tall ornamental brick chimney stacks which towered above the slate roof.

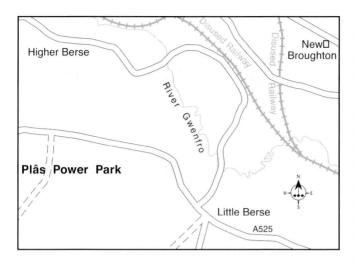

Mary Fitzhugh, wife of Thomas Fitzhugh of Portland Place, Middlesex, was the only child of William Lloyd of Plas Power and she was the sole heiress to the estate on her father's death. Their son Thomas Lloyd Fitzhugh inherited the estate from his father and in 1858 carried out a remodelling scheme to the house, enlarging it at the same time. The architect who carried out the work was John Gibson, a native of Conway, and a well-known sculptor.

At the same time that William Lloyd was building the new house, it was decided to enclose the parkland by building a massive stone wall on the boundary to the road. The miners from the nearby village had for many years had the freedom of using the parkland for walking and racing their greyhounds. This stone wall was going to put a stop to their sporting activities. When the stonemasons arrived to start building the wall, they met with strong opposition from the miners and, after the masons had finished work for the day and gone home, the miners would return at nightfall and demolish the wall that had been built during the day. The work became so disrupted that the owners of the estate had to engage the services of the Militia from the barracks at Wrexham. The Militia set up camp on the parkland and kept guard on the wall until it was completed.

Just prior to the war (1939-45), it was discovered that the house was badly affected with dry rot, which was widely spread throughout the building. The cost for the eradication and repair of the damage was so great that the owner decided to vacate the property and move into the large house of the farm bailiff on the home farm. The house at Plas Power was left vacant until it was demolished in 1951. Col. Thomas Fitzhugh was the grandson of the last Lloyd of Plas Power and father of the present Fitzhugh. His name is mentioned as having served as churchwarden at St Giles Parish Church in 1828-29. In 1946 the Plas Power estate was taken over for an extensive open-cast mining operation for coal and it was a number of years before the land was reinstated.

Plas-y-Brain estate dates back to the medi-eval times and was situated on the outskirts of Treuddyn Village, with extensive views over the Vale of Mold. It formed part of the farm build-ings and had a rugged appearance. It was built in random rubble limestone. It was built in the early 16th century with additional work added later in the century. There were other additions carried out in more recent times. The house was partly half-timber construction with cruck trusses. The central roof truss was open to the roof space and the tie-beam had braces. The purlins had cham-fered wind braces and looked most decorative with the quatrefoil set above the tie-beam.

A large lateral chimney stack was added in the late 16th century, the top of which had been extended at a later date. The other three chimney stacks had been built in brick. Originally this type of dwelling would most likely have had a thatched roof, but in the early 19th century the roof was slated.

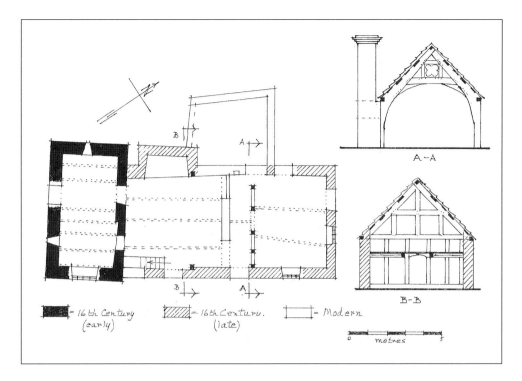

= 16th Century (early)

= 16th Century (late)

= Modern

A–A

B–B

0   metres   5

The house was built in three phases as shown on the plan. The internal partitions were exposed timber studding with wattle and daub infill. The ceilings to the rooms were open beam ceilings with the main beams stop chamfered.

The dwelling reached a stage when the building required a great deal of money to be spent on the fabric to bring it up to present-day standards. A new house was built on a different site to replace the old dwelling. The old house was left vacant, soon became derelict and collapsed in the 1980s.

The street in which The Priory was situated was originally the carriage drive to Bryn-y-Ffynnon House. It was about the early 18th century when the house was built, on the site opposite the lodge belonging to Bryn-y-Ffynnon House. The family had owned a house on the same site as far back as 1661. When The Priory was built the driveway was widened and became known as Priory Street. The street finished at the end of The Priory garden and it then narrowed to form the pathway that led down to the rear of the Old Vicarage.

The house was never a priory, but during that era it was fashionable for the affluent clientele to call their houses by impressive names. The house was built in the Queen Anne style of the period; slate roof with stout brick chimney stacks towering above the roof. It was built in a mellow brick with stone features, the plan of the house was "T" shaped and had been extended at a later date. It was a two and a half storey building with three dormer windows set in the roof of the front elevation. The Priory was set in a well laid out garden of considerable size with mature trees. To the south, the garden bordered that of the Old Vicarage. To the north, the garden bordered on to the property situated in Hope Street and, to the east side of the garden, was a bowling green. In 1870 part of the garden was sold off for development. On the north side of the house was constructed a carriage drive and halfway down the drive, to the rear of the house, were a pair of ornamental wrought-iron gates with stone piers. These gave access to the cobbled yard at the rear of the property where the stables, coach-house and other outbuildings were situated.

The Priory was built as a town house for the Edwards family of Stansty Isa. They were an ancient wealthy family from the Stansty area. Edward ap David ap Robert gave

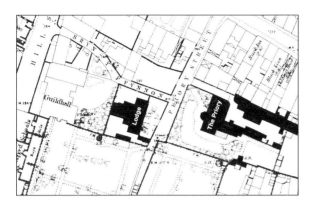

his name to his descendants, the Edwards of Stansty Isa. He was the grandson of Robert ap Jenkins of Stansty Uchaf. The Edwards family had played an important part in the social life of the town. David Edwards had served as churchwarden at St Giles Parish Church, Wrexham, in 1663-64. He was the son of David Edwards of the same address, who had married Dorothy, the daughter of Thomas Goldsmith of Wrexham, a wealthy landowner, and there were three children to the marriage. David died at the age of 63 years and was buried in Rhuddlan churchyard.

One of the Edwards daughters, Jane, married Thomas Baker in 1662; he was a Captain in the Royal Army and he died in 1672. John Edwards the younger was born in 1687, died in 1727 and was buried at Gresford. He was the son of John Edwards senior; he also served as churchwarden at St Giles in 1712-13.

Between the years 1699 and 1783, the Priory was occupied by Peter Edwards who died there; he was the last in the male line of the Edwards family. After his death the Priory was let on a lease to Madam Yonge, who was one of the family of Yonge from Bryn Iorcyn. She lived at the Priory until her death and, during the latter part of Madam Yonge's stay at the Priory, she shared the house with her companion, Miss Barbara Speed, who was a sister to Griffith Speed of 58, Hope Street, Wrexham, where he had an ironmongery business. In 1760 he held the office of High Sheriff of the County. In the year 1808 Miss Letitia Eyton occupied The Priory until her death in 1837. She was the third daughter of the Rev. John and Penelope Eyton of Leeswood Hall; there were many children to the marriage.

After the occupation of Miss Eyton, The Priory was sold to Charles Poyser, a mercer of Wrexham. After this period the property became the offices of Sir Evan Morris & Co, solicitors. At the turn of the century the Priory was demolished to make way for a shopping development.

Pwll-yr-Uwd was a large Elizabethan house dating back to the 15th century, situated in the low-lying area in Wrexham Regis off the Holt Road. It was a two and a half storey building built in half-timber construction with wattle and daub infill, the lower part of the house being built in random rubble stonework. The gables were decorative and the roof was of slate with tall bold brick chimney stacks. Close to the house were a cluster of farm buildings and near the homestead was a large pool of water from which the house derived its name. Most of the land surrounding the holding had been the common grazing land for the district, but was enclosed under licence in 1581.

Pwll-yr-Uwd was a small estate of 70 acres which had been built for the Puleston family who had settled at Hafod-y-Wern. The estate came into their possession in 1580 and later, in 1661, came into the possession of Hugh Puleston and his wife Jane, who was the daughter of John Evans of Llwyn Egryn. Hugh lived at Pwll-yr-Uwd until his death in 1666 and Jane, his widow, lived on in the house until her death in 1686. During this period the farm was let to a tenant farmer who lived in part of the house with Jane.

The estate was then inherited by Robert Puleston and his wife who was the daughter of Ambrose Lewis (the first). The Lewis family had grown wealthy through marrying into various rich estates. When Richard Puleston inherited Pwll-yr-Uwd estate, he was the fourth son of the third wife of John Puleston of Hafod-y-Wern, who was the grandson of Madoc Puleston of Bersham. Richard's wife was the daughter of Meredith ap Thomas of Porthamel in Anglesey. The estate remained in the Puleston family for many years, until 1714 when the male line died out. Mary Puleston inherited Pwll-yr-Uwd and married Peter Potter, a book-binder from Chester.

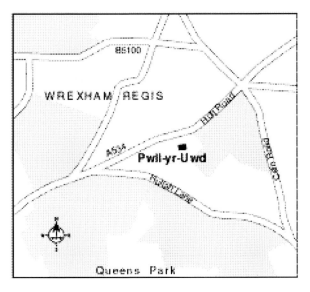

In 1784 the estate passed into the ownership of Robert Bamford-Hesketh of Bromford Hall in Lancashire, who had married Frances, daughter of John Lloyd, Vicar of Llanasa. Previously he had been curate at St Giles Parish Church, Wrexham from 1748 to 1759. The Rev. John Lloyd was the son of William Lloyd of Gwrych estate, Abergele. He had married Eleanor in 1748, daughter of Ambrose Lewis (the second). Thus through marriage all the estates of the Ambrose Lewis family came to John and Eleanor Lloyd, which included Pwll-yr-Uwd.

In 1768, it appears that the Pwll-yr-Uwd estate was now being let to various tenant farmers; John Hughes was one of the first tenants to occupy the farm. He farmed the holding until his death in 1775 and was buried at Wrexham. His son, who was also John Hughes, inherited the tenancy and according to the Rate Book, was still farming there in 1788. John Hughes junior, in 1784 married in London Mrs E. Cooke, widow of John Cooke, of Swith's Place, Flintshire. They lived at Pwll-yr-Uwd for about two years, when Mrs E. Cooke died in November 1786 and was buried at Wrexham.

The Pwll-yr-Uwd estate was inherited by Edward Holt of Chester, through his marriage to Maria, another daughter of the Rev. John Lloyd of Gwrych, Abergele. She was the grand-daughter of the 3rd Ambrose Lewis. During the period around 1816, Charles Davies, a farmer, held the lease. The house and buildings at Pwll-yr-Uwd were demolished in the late 19th century and on the site a Council housing estate called Spring Lodge was built. The holding was known as Spring Lodge as far back as 1810, and was sometime spelt "Pwll-yr-Ywd".

TY'N-Y-CAEAU FARM, AND THE DOG KENNEL
CAIA LANE, WREXHAM

This historical farmhouse is better known as Caia Farm and was situated at the end of a rough cart track, now known as Caia Road. The house dates back to 1668, when it was recorded in the Rate Book of that period. The farmhouse was on an elevated site overlooking the River Gwenfro; the farm buildings were situated at a lower level east of the farmhouse. The house was built in half-timber construction with brick infill and the roof was in slate. The elevations have been stucco rendered at a later date; this was a typical undertaking – when the timber showed signs of rot, they covered it to hide a multitude of sins. Caia Farm house is still standing to this day; it was renovated and

converted into a public house in about 1973, but the interior has changed very little.

The Caia Farm formed part of the Hafod-y-Wern estate which was owned by the Puleston family. During the period between 1704 and 1738 the property was the home of John Jones, the noted almanac maker. He was a member of the congregation of the New Meeting House in Wrexham. The Rev. John Kenrick, who was the minister at the time, baptised his children, Margaret, John and Hugh. John Jones died at Caia Farm in 1738 and was buried in the Dissenters Graveyard situated in Rhosddu Road.

The neighbouring property, known as The Dog Kennel, also belonged to the same estate and was farmed by a tenant, Thomas Jones, a successful market gardener. His family had been connected with The Dog Kennel for over a hundred years; the house was of the cottage type with limited building accommodation and was joined to the house. The property derived its name from the time when the hounds were housed in the building for the local hunt. Thomas Jones married Harriet, daughter of Thomas Roberts, a maltster of Wrexham, and their son, the Rev. Edward Jones, became a noted local Wesleyan Chapel preacher. The Dog Kennel was also built in half-timber construction with brick infill. The area of the holding was in the region of 38 acres and was eventually demolished to make way for the Wrexham Gas Works. An apothecary who lived and had his shop in the High Street, Wrexham, moved to The Dog Kennel in 1782. At the end of the 19th century, a cobbler by the name of Samuel Bradburn was the last tenant to occupy it. He was a well-known local Wesleyan preacher.

By the year 1844 the area of land to Caia Farm had been reduced to about 19 acres, about 19 acres having been sold off for housing development. Robert Warral, who kept

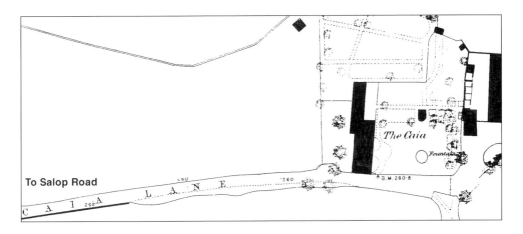

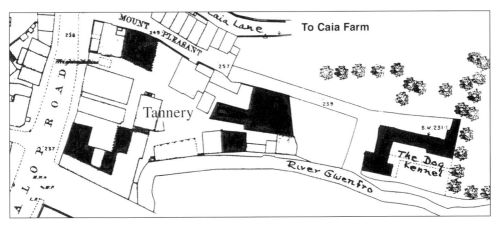

The Red Lion public house in the High Street, Wrexham, was a tenant at Caia Farm for a number of years. His name is mentioned in the register at St Giles Parish Church as having served as churchwarden in 1764-65. He died at the farm in 1786 and was buried at Wrexham. Another tenant at Caia Farm was John Valentine. At one time he had kept the public house known as The Three Pigeons in the High Street, Wrexham, now called The Red Lion. John Valentine was also a grazier, who had moved from a large house in Hope Street, Wrexham.

In 1825 the land agent who managed the Hafod-y-Wern estate, Bryan Cooke, sold Caia Farm and The Dog Kennel to a Chester Solicitor. At a later date, Bryan Cooke became a partner in the firm of charted surveyors and land agents, Cooke and Arkwright, High Street, Mold. On the death of Mr Potts, the Chester solicitor, his daughter inherited the two properties. In 1876 she sold the two farms to an Irishman by the name of Ebenezer Pike of Bessborough, County Cork. He died at Caia Farm in 1883 and on his death his widow sold the two farms to Benjamin Piercy of Marchwiel Hall. Part of the land was used for the extension of the Wrexham to Connah's Quay Railway; the rest of the land was developed for domestic dwellings. Benjamin Piercy died at Marchwiel in 1888, aged 61 years.

The house was originally built for Edward James, a "currier" from Pen-y-bryn, about 1742 (a currier was a person who dressed and coloured tanned leather). Beyond that date there is no mention of Well House in the Rate Book of that period. Well House had played a great part in the social and commercial life of the town, as it had been one of the principal houses in the township of Wrexham.

Edward James appeared to have had a tragic family life. His wife Mary died in 1749 at the early age of 29, their son John died at the early age of 22 in 1766, and they also had two daughters who died in infancy. Edward James died at Well House in 1772, aged 66 years. During his life he was a regular supporter of the parish church of St Giles where he served as churchwarden in 1737-38.

Well House then came into the possession of Thomas Edwards, who was also a tanner in Pen-y-bryn. He worked the tannery previously owned by his relative William Edwards. William Edwards had lived for a number of years at a large house known as The Palace, situated on the site where the Cambrian Brewery once stood. He also served as churchwarden at the parish church in 1776-77; he died in 1797. William Edwards was related to the Edwards family living in the Stansty area. He had two sons, Thomas and John, who both lived at Well House. John Edwards inherited the Well House estate on his father's death. Thomas Edwards became a wealthy man and was known locally as "The King".

John Edwards was also a currier and lived at Well House for a number of years and died there in 1804. He served as churchwarden at St Giles church in 1807-08, and was known locally as "The Duke".

The house was built in brick with stone features and was L-shaped in plan. The gables projected above the slate roof and finished with coping stones, being supported at eaves level with moulded corbel stones. Under the eaves were two courses of corbelled brick and a brick chimney stack sited at each end of the roof. The property was situated in Well Square, in the centre of which was the town well. The well was surrounded on three sides by a stone wall, while the open side gave access to stone steps leading down to the spring. It was stated in the records that during the winter months the flow from the spring was 2,000 gallons per hour; the overflow from the spring was piped through wooden pipes to the River Gwenfro (the Town Brook) in Brook Street.

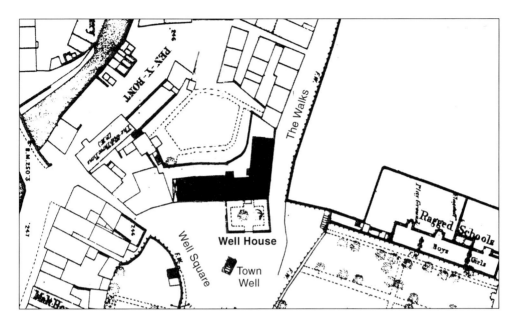

The front garden to Well House projected into the square about twenty feet and was surrounded by a brick ornamental wall. A stout pair of brick gate piers supported an ornamental wrought-iron gate. This part of the property was in the Parish of Esclusham (detached) while the house itself was in the parish of Wrexham Abbot. Adjoining the house, a large brick building comprising of a barn, stable and coach-house with hay loft above, looked out over a cobbled-stone yard.

In 1895 Well House was sold to the railway company to make way for the construction of the Ellesmere Railway and the house was used as offices for the railway company. The property was demolished in 1896, together with other historical buildings in the area – what a great loss to the town!

The original house built on the site of Yspytty Isaf was of half-timber construction with a thatched roof. It dated back to the early part of the 17th century and was
built by a wealthy farming family by the name of Hughes, who farmed on a large farm in
the Stansty area. The same family had a number of rented properties in various parts of
the town. The house was built as an investment property and let to various short stay tenants. In the early days the street leading to Queen's Square was known as "Sputty Street".

One of the early tenants was John Lewis, who was one of the leading attorneys-at-law
in the town and carried on his business by the name of John Lewis & Son. His home was
at The Lodge, Rhosddu. He terminated his tenancy at Yspytty Isaf in 1742, died in the
July of 1762, aged 82 years, and was buried in Rhosddu graveyard. He married Catherin
in 1740, a daughter of John Broadfoot.

The property was leased to Thomas Hayman, another attorney-at-law, whose tenancy
ran from 1742 to 1747 when he moved to a house called "Ty-Meredith", in Chester
Street. He married Eleanor, one of the daughters of John Puleston of Pickhill Hall, by
whom he had four children. Anne, his only daughter, held the post of "Privy Purse" to
the then Princess of Wales, Queen Caroline. His younger son, Watkin, was disabled, but
was known for his tremendous sense of humour and wit. Thomas Hayman died in 1783
and was buried at Gresford.

Yspytty Isaf was purchased by Vincent Price, a noted surgeon in the town, who ran
his practice from the house. His first marriage was to Mrs Catherine Broadfoot in
1740 but she died in September 1746. His second marriage was to Mary Edwards of
Croesnewydd Hall in 1747; she was a friend and companion of Mary Myddelton who
resided at Croesnewydd Hall. Mary Price, his wife, died in May 1761 and was buried at
Wrexham, but Vincent Price lived on at Yspytty Isaf until his death, which was just after
he had rebuilt the house in grand scale in 1786. The spacious garden was landscaped;
this was situated behind the houses in Lambpit Street. At the lower end of the garden
was a circular summer-house with a thatched roof (see map). The front elevation to the
new house was built in a dressed buff-coloured sandstone with tall sliding sash windows,
and incorporated in the elevation were two bow windows. The rear elevation was built

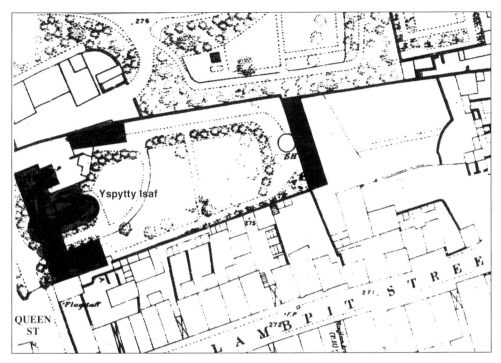

in brick and faced the delightful garden. At the north side of the house was the cobbled courtyard, giving access to the coach-house and stables.

In 1789 the estate was purchased by John Evans, a mercer and clothier whose shop was situated at 36 and 37, High Street, Wrexham. He lived at Yspytty Isaf until his death in 1796. The house was then let to Watkin Hayman for a period of about three years, until he died in 1799 and was buried at Worthenbury. His wife lived on at Yspytty Isaf until her death in 1805.

The estate was now inherited by John Evan's nephew, John Burton, who was a retired gentleman who lived in the house until his death in 1813. He was buried in the Dissenters burial ground in Rhosddu Road.

In 1821 the property was then inherited by the Rev. John Pearce through his wife's family. He lived at Yspytty Isaf until his bankruptcy, which happened in 1853 (this is mentioned in the section on Broughton Hall, Southsea, see page 14).

The property was then leased to a bank with living accommodation, but after a short tenancy the bank went into liquidation. The estate was put on the market and sold to a John Lewis, a solicitor who used the premises for his office.

Yspytty Isaf had played a great and important part in the social life of the town, and also had connections with the commercial life of Wrexham. In 1898 Yspytty Isaf estate was purchased by the Wrexham Town Council. Shortly after this the house was demolished to make way for a Council development.

The name "Yspytty" means Hospice.